what to expect when you're accepted

An African American Christian's Guide to College

Christopher Michael Jones

Foreword by Floyd H. Flake

JUDSON PRESS
PUBLISHERS SINCE 1824

VALLEY FORGE, PA

What to Expect When You're Accepted:
An African American Christian's Guide to College
© 2007 by Judson Press, Valley Forge, PA 19482-0851
All rights reserved.

Introduction © 2007 by Karen Jackson-Weaver

Library of Congress Cataloging-in-Publication Data

Jones, Christopher Michael.
    What to expect when you're accepted : an African American Christian's guide to college / Christopher Michael Jones ; foreword by Floyd H. Flake. — 1st ed.
      p. cm.
    ISBN 978-0-8170-1517-6 (pbk. : alk. paper) 1. College student orientation—United States—Handbooks, manuals, etc. 2. African American students—Handbooks, manuals, etc. 3. African American students—Attitudes. I. Title.
    LB2343.32.J646 2007
    378.1′982996073—dc22

2007002847

Printed on recycled paper in the U.S.A.

First Edition, 2007.

Dedicated to the two sacred jewels
that God has given to me:
my beloved
Jordan Matthew and Taylor Elise Jones

Acknowledgments

It would be impossible to thank all the persons whose lives and ministries have had an impact on my life, but let me express my gratitude here to a few of the many who have.

I am thankful to Rebecca Irwin-Diehl for her generous invitation to become a part of the Judson Press family. Kim Shimer, Gale Tull, Frank Seawright, Lisa Blair, and the rest of the staff at Judson Press have made this process rich and meaningful for me.

I would like to thank Rutgers University professors Mia Bay and Mark Colby for helping me to shape critical reflections on ideas related to African American history and moral philosophy. I have benefited richly by their mentorship, and I appreciate their contributions to my intellectual development.

I offer special thanks to Bishop Donald Hilliard Jr. and Dr. Bernadette Glover-Williams. Both have extended their mentoring hands and resources toward me. You can only become what you know, and what I know comes partly from what they have taught me. Thanks, Cathedral family!

I give thanks also to Grandma G and Big Daddy. I could not think of better grandparents. Not only have they given me a rich African heritage to hold on to, but they sowed a seed of faith into my childhood that has now come to full bloom. Thank you so much for loving me.

Thanks also go to Aunt Martha, Uncle Kermit, Auntie B, Auntie M, Aunt Deborah, and the entire Mayfield family. You have each offered tremendous love and support to me over the years. Phyllis, you are a blessing!

To my mother and father, Sheila Mayfield and James T. Jones Jr., thanks for sharing with me practical illustrations from the lessons life has taught you. Both of you have made me stronger. I could not be the husband and father that I am without you. God bless you both!

Mom Etheridge and the Etheridge family, I bless the Lord because of you. You have made things happen for me in countless ways. Brittany, you have no excuse—you have this manual and you have my love. Dare to be great in your first year of college!

To the Princeton 3: It is what it is. Destiny waits for no one. I encourage you to embrace whatever it is God has called you to be. Your people, our people, are depending on you.

Rev. Martha Simmons, you already know much of what I could say. The words thank you only abbreviate the length of the good that could be spoken of you.

Finally, to my wife and best friend, Nikki Michelle Jones. Wow! None of this would be possible without your unending love and support. Much in the way the African violet blooms in the mountain cloud forest of Mbololo, Kenya, your presence seems to make life's bumps and turns much smoother than what they could be. You are a blessing to me.

Jordan and Taylor, your father loves you. I pray that my efforts serve you well. Remember to tell your children's children, all things are possible through Christ who strengthens us (Philippians 4:13).

And to Kenny and Franklin, I love you, bros!

Contents

FRESHMAN YEAR
Getting Settled

SOPHOMORE YEAR
Getting Serious

Foreword

What do you expect from a book called *What to Expect When You're Accepted: An African American Christian's Guide to College?* Well, I'll tell you what you're going to find: a faith-filled survival guide to navigating the obstacle-ridden years of undergraduate education. You couldn't ask for a better travel guide than Rev. Christopher Michael Jones. Following the divots left in the sand from the footsteps of persons such as Howard Thurman and Samuel DeWitt Proctor, Rev. Jones has traveled the narrow path for a new generation and knows what it takes to press on toward the high calling we have in Christ Jesus.

In this convenient handbook, you will find for each year of the traditional undergraduate program solid advice about forming and maintaining solid relationships, gentle warnings about avoiding common pitfalls, practical counsel about staying physically healthy, concrete tips for achieving academic success, and last but not least, spiritual wisdom for each stage of the collegial journey.

Don't plan to read this book cover to cover in one sitting, even though it is concise and plain speaking enough to do just that. Make this book your constant companion throughout your college experience, and believe that the Spirit of God who sustained its author will also sustain you until your Graduation Day—and beyond!

Rev. Dr. Floyd H. Flake
President, Wilberforce University
Senior Pastor, The Greater Allen AME Cathedral
Jamaica, New York
Commissioner, President's Commission on
Excellence in Special Education

Preface

Interest isn't ability and skill doesn't guarantee success. Games and gadgets come with directions because their makers realize that wanting to do something and being able to do it are two different things. "Want to" and "how to" aren't two sides of the same coin. LeBron James—"King James"—may have flair with a basketball, but he still has a coach. Regardless of talent, motivation, and opportunity, if you want to win, a coach is needed.

When it comes to college, Christopher Jones is the coach, and what's in your hand right now is the playbook. *What to Expect When You're Accepted: An African American Christian's Guide to College* provides encouragement and practical insight in each chapter. Because I have watched the author himself juggle-balance the interests and requirements of family, school, work, and self-care without becoming shipwrecked—trust me when I say the counsel in this guide is reliable. Read it. Think about it. Share it with a friend. Just, whatever you do, don't shelve the information that's here.

There's an impressive, strikingly lit four-lane bridge in Perth Amboy. Boats and barges quietly pass beneath it. It's called "Victory

Bridge." College is a bridge that makes it possible to go from where you are to where you want to be. So, set yourself up to succeed. God has plans for you, and every last one of them is good news. Let the Holy Spirit speak to you and empower you. Cross the bridge, my friend. Destiny awaits you.

Rev. Dr. Bernadette Glover-Williams
Executive Pastor
Cathedral International—Second Baptist Church
Perth Amboy, New Jersey
Preacher in Residence
New Brunswick Theological Seminary

Introduction

Congratulations! My dear sisters and brothers in Christ, I salute you for the achievements and accomplishments which have led you to this point in your academic career—acceptance to college. Now, get ready! You are about to embark upon a very important journey—one of the most important pilgrimages of your life. Some of you may be first-generation college students while others may come from a family with a legacy of college graduates. Regardless of your status, this book is here to help you succeed. God has blessed you with a wonderful opportunity to pursue your studies at an institution of higher learning, and this guide will provide you with practical steps to achieve your goals.

I recall walking on campus one crisp autumn day during my first semester as a freshman at Princeton University. I was cruising as usual, and then all of sudden, I stopped. I looked up past the trees at the clouds, and as I paused and marveled at God's creations, I remember feeling the omnipotent presence of God. I was away from home, far from everything and everyone that I knew and was familiar with. Here I was in New Jersey with no family and few friends. Immediately, I remember the comforting presence of the Holy Spirit assuring me, "My beloved Karen, remember God will never leave you nor forsake you" (see Deuteronomy 31:8). And I know the same to be true for you. It is normal to be a little nervous about college and what your future holds. Whether you attend school out of state or in state, you are blessed because you have this guide to provide you with excellent strategies to thrive during your college career.

While I was not as fortunate as you to have a guide specifically targeted to African American Christians bound for college, I did have friends, family, and others who edified me and encouraged me to persevere. And by God's grace I did. Four years after that crisp autumn day, I completed my BA at Princeton and then went on to obtain my master's degree from Harvard University. After working for several years in the field of education, I returned to school and received my MA, MPhil, and PhD from Columbia University. I can tell you that when I arrived on Princeton University's campus, I was not planning to get a PhD. In fact, I was 100 percent sure I wanted to be a lawyer. Trust me when I tell you that your college years allow you the freedom to pursue your intellectual interests. Please do not be held captive to doing what sounds good or what others think you should do. Seek the wise counsel of professors, clergy, and upperclassmen, and be prayerful and contemplative about the opportunities that God presents to you.

As a history major at Princeton, I was horrified and enraged when I read primary source documents that bore witness to our African ancestors' brutal enslavement, disenfranchisement, and continuous denial of educational opportunities. However, what constantly gave me a sense of hope was learning that generations of our foremothers and forefathers paved the way for us to have the opportunity to attend the colleges and universities of our choice in the twenty-first century.

Remember, you are following in the footsteps of trailblazers such as Alexander Lucius Twilight, who is noted to have been the first African American to receive a baccalaureate degree from a college or university in the United States. He was born in 1795 in Vermont and graduated from Middlebury College in 1823. Honoring his Christian tradition, he became a licensed preacher in the Presbyterian Church, and he also served as an educator and school administrator. Twilight is also considered the first African American to serve in a state level public office. In 1836, he was elected to be a legislator in Vermont's House of Representatives.[1]

Other pioneers such as Dr. Susan McKinney Steward inspired me. Dr. Steward is recorded as the first African American woman to receive her medical school degree in New York State, and the third in the nation. In 1870 she graduated from New York Medical School for Women, and if that weren't enough, Dr. Steward was the class valedictorian! During her career, she spoke in the community, at schools, and at local churches about myriad topics such as her specialized training in homeopathy.[2] Understand, my sisters and brothers, that you have an inheritance of intellectual excellence! God has opened this door for you despite whatever challenges or situations you may have faced to get here.

Now that you are headed to college, we want you to stay and **graduate.** The U.S. Department of Education reported that in 2005 some 127,844 African Americans graduated with four-year degrees from colleges and universities throughout the United States. That figure represents the highest number of bachelor's degrees earned by African Americans in the nation's history.[3] However, a recent article in *The Journal of Blacks in Higher Education* reports that while the large increase in bachelor's degrees earned by blacks is encouraging, "it must always be remembered that only about two out of every five black students who enroll as freshmen in college go on to graduate within six years from the same institution they entered."[4] Fortunately for you, *What to Expect When You're Accepted: An African American Christian's Guide to College* is packed full of useful tips to help you succeed and have a fruitful college experience.

Please take time and reflect on the golden nuggets of advice that this guide offers. Underline! Highlight! You have an opportunity to commune with this book, not just be a passive reader. I encourage you to accentuate useful points that speak to your spirit. Make your own notes in the margins. Keep a journal or a list of ideas so that you have a written record of your goals and future plans. Refer to *What to Expect When You're Accepted* often, and feel free to skip around versus reading in consecutive order, page by page. My prayer for you today is that God's grace, power, and mercy will be unleashed in your life in a mighty way to bless you, equip you, and provide you with all of the strength, stamina, and knowledge you need to successfully complete your undergraduate degree. Remember, you are on the winning side; if God is for you, who can be against you? (see Romans 8:31). So in God's name, press on!

Karen Jackson-Weaver, PhD
Executive Director
New Jersey Amistad Commission[5]
January 1, 2007

Notes

1. www.twilightandreason.com.

2. http://www.lkwdpl.org/wihohio/stew-sus.htm.

3. *The Journal of Blacks in Higher Education* (JBHE), no. 54, winter 2006/2007. http://www.jbhe.com/news_views/54_bachelors-degree-highs.html.

4. Ibid.

5. The Amistad Commission was established by the State of New Jersey in 2002 with the goal of incorporating African American history into the curriculum of New Jersey's public schools. Members work to increase awareness of the African slave trade, slavery in America, and the contemporary vestiges of enslavement in modern America. For more information, visit www.theamistadcommission.com. *Please note the statements contained here are the viewpoints of Dr. Jackson-Weaver and not the official view of the NJ Amistad Commission.

FRESHMAN YEAR

Getting Settled

1

Exploring New Friendships

Okay, here we are. You did it. Welcome to college. You have just arrived on campus. By now you are in your new room with your new roommate and have checked off items from the "What to Bring & What Not to Bring" list. You've brought posters, flip-flops, laundry detergent, the laptop, the TV, and the Sony PlayStation III, but you forgot the extension cord, laundry basket, and your favorite Beyonce CD. Or perhaps you are returning to college as a nighttime commuter. In which case, you remembered to bring your photo ID to register for class, but you forgot to bring the checkbook and the ATM card. Don't worry. Do not panic. Whether you are entering college for the first time or returning after a long hiatus, one thing will become obviously clear to you: you cannot do this alone.

You will need *people*, *prayer*, and *patience* to get you through your freshman year of college. That's right: *people*, *prayer*, and *patience*. So, turn the cell phone off for a minute. Lower the volume on the MP3 and log off of MySpace.com. Let's talk about this. If we are going to make it through college together, there is much we need to discuss. Let's begin by talking about *why* you need to explore new friendships at all. Are you ready?

You Need People

It is not God's intention that you travel along life's pathways alone. Remember Genesis 2:18, "It is not good for the man to be alone"? God wasn't only talking about marriage. Human beings were created in the divine image—and God exists in eternal fellowship as the Trinity. We are created for comparable fellowship—and nowhere are relationships more important than in exploring new territory at college.

Trust me—you will not have the answer to every statistics exam, nor will you always have enough cash for the midnight snack at the 7-Eleven. Do you want a part-time job? Friends usually have the scoop on such matters. Yes, you have Jesus, and yes, Jesus is your best friend. However, Jesus desires that we fellowship with one another. It is through our friendships that we learn more about who God is. Friendships enable us to grow, mature, and stretch in our capacity to love.

That being established, the next question is, how do we go about forming new friendships? This is where prayer and patience come into the picture.

You Need Prayer

I have found that making the transition to college can be stressful. By now, I'm sure you would agree. Yes, we are all entering NYU, Princeton, Spelman, and the local community college, but we do so leaving behind so many familiar friends, family, and foes. Sure, we will learn new things, explore new places, and meet new people. However, if we do not prepare for the quick changes that come our way—and trust me they will come—stress and anxiety could overtake us. This is why we need *prayer.*

Making new friends always seems to be the hardest part of the process for entering into college. Admit it. We need to feel accepted from time to time. You need it. I need it. We all need it. That's why we buy the clothes we wear and do the things we do. We want to be Christian, and we want to be affirmed. And that's okay. That's our human nature. Of course, outward appearances never reveal who we really are, but you get the point. We all need meaningful relationships to carry us through. I've found that *prayer* settles the nerves when I meet new people. *Prayer* helps us determine which friendships are best for us. So, as you pray, I'll list a few pointers on how to explore new friendships:

- Keep your head up, not down. There will always be persons on campus who appear to be better equipped at making friends than you. Please do not bury yourself behind your headphones and new portable DVD Player! Maintain a positive attitude. Keep your head up. A good happy smile and an alert response to an unexpected question will always make for a good presentation of who you are in Christ Jesus.

- Maintain a healthy Christian perspective on life. We are what we think, and we say what we really believe. If you think of yourself as being a quality person, you will attract quality people. It's as simple as that. Fill your mind with Scripture, poems, and essays that reflect positive outlooks on life. Avoid images that distort who you are as an African American Christian. Dress for success. Likeminded people attract like-minded people. If you walk or talk trash, you will attract trash.

- Be true to your word. The worst thing you can do as you explore this new world is break a promise. If you want to gain a friend, be a friend. Do what you say. Say what you mean. Keep your friend's private conversations and confidences close to your heart while you pray. As the saying goes, "Loose lips sink ships." So, watch your mouth. Stay holy.

You Need Patience

I've also discovered that developing new relationships takes time. Be *patient*. Real friendships do not happen overnight. In fact, nothing happens overnight. I know, "Welcome Week" festivities, opening orientation, and instant messaging all offer intense and immediate connections, right? Hear me out. Read the life story of the acclaimed *American Idol* winner Fantasia Barrino. Through much pain and many setbacks, Fantasia's voice matured over time. Friendships grow and mature over time as people share their life experiences together. Too often we call people friends without having shared any real life experiences with them. We hit their MySpace site, share pictures over the Internet, and *pow!* we think we're friends. Friendships do not just happen. They develop, evolve, and grow.

Remember, trust is a critical ingredient in any relationship, and time alone allows trust to emerge between friends. Trust will develop as friends grow close together over time. Here are a few more pointers to consider as you explore new friendships:

- Be yourself. Don't front and don't be pushy! Never try to be more than what you are. Give people space. People need time and space to determine when and if they will share their life story with you. The idea is to develop real friendships over time and not create loose superficial acquaintances that only help you short-term.

- "No" means "no." This phrase applies to friendships as much as it does to dating relationships. If your friend decides to set boundaries within the relationship, respect those lines. Some people don't want to talk to you about their spouse or their new dating partner. They may even share their personal information with another person. So what? It's not necessarily personal. People look for multiple relationships because they're human. If that private part of their life is off limits, respect their wishes. Maintain a sense of *patience* and discernment in the matter.

- Just turn the page. I've heard this point expressed by my senior pastor, Bishop Donald Hilliard Jr., a million times. Sometimes you just have to "turn the page," and let the things you don't understand take care of themselves. There will be days when your friend just doesn't want to be bothered. Don't take it personally. Let a day go by. Maybe two. Then call them back to make sure they are okay. Good friends stick together, even in the bad times.
- Stay connected to the community of faith. Whether you maintain a relationship with your home church and pastor, make a new connection with a campus ministry or college chaplain, or begin to visit local churches in the area, don't lose sight of the value of remaining connected with the Body of Christ on earth. There you can find people who share your faith, will pray with and for you, and encourage you in patience and wisdom as you form new friendships at college. (We will talk more about the vital importance of identifying and partnering with a local church in chapter 10.)

As you prayerfully explore new friendships, remember to do so patiently. You need people and people need you. Be open and let your friends learn who you are. Remember to be honest and to be sensitive to the needs of others. God will take care of the rest. For a quick meditation, here's a Scripture taken from the Book of Proverbs: "A friend loves at all times, and a brother is born for adversity" (Proverbs 17:17, NIV). Think on it as we go to the next chapter.

2

Discovering New Boundaries

Let me guess. I bet you never expected such a quick turn-around when you arrived on campus. You have a headache, a blister on your finger, and your feet hurt don't they? Do you see why you need *people, prayer,* and *patience?* Not only are you challenged to adjust to new friendships, but now you face the daunting task of familiarizing yourself with your new surroundings. Whirlwind "Welcome Week" check-ins, circus-like opening orientations, and "New-Student" talent shows are all created by college administrations to convey one idea: "Welcome to the college experience, the place from which you will begin a life's journey of discovery!"

First things first: You'll need to gain a quick understanding of the way things work on your campus. Not only will your mind be challenged to grasp the fundamentals of statistics, psychology, and American history, but you'll also need to know how to locate the office of your academic advisor, the library, campus security, a student health-care facility, and a local variety store where you can resupply your personal toiletry items when the stash gets low. So, here are a few check-points you should take into consideration as you feel your way through your new surroundings:

An Academic Advisor (Guidance or Career Counselor)

- Who is it? An adult representative provided by the college or university to whom you, as a student, can turn for guidance on how to plan an undergraduate academic program.
- What does an advisor do?
  1. Ensure that you transition well into the new curriculum, whether you are entering as a new high-school grad, a transfer student, or a returning upperclassman.
  2. Help you become familiar with course offerings and other opportunities that breed individual academic success.
  3. Assist you in identifying and declaring a major and in structuring the rest of your college courses.

The College Library

- What is it? A treasure trove of information and a refuge for quiet study, usually located in a central area on campus and accessible most hours of the day and night.
- What can be found there?
  1. Books, books, and more books!
  2. A selection of current magazines and newspapers to keep you up to date on world events as well as old publications stored in the stacks or on microfilm, microfiche, or electronic archives
  3. A collection of professional and academic journals rich in data for research projects and papers
  4. Research guides and databases to guide you in your search for general knowledge or specific facts
  5. Digital collections and e-journals to secure archived resources
  6. Area and regional catalogues of other research facilities, many of which may have exchanges with your college library
  7. Computers with Internet access (often restricted for research use)

- How can you use it?
  1. Retreat to special reading rooms or study cubicles for a quiet (and secure) study space away from your living or social areas.
  2. Explore its shelves and archives in your leisure time or when you need to escape from the academic grind—reading can be recreation as well as education!
  3. Make friends with the librarian and other specialized clerks and research assistants, who will be an invaluable help for your research projects and personal development.
  4. Stay abreast of current events and emerging ideas by taking advantage of the library's copies of newspapers, magazines, and journals.

Campus Security

- Who are they? A private security force (sometimes called "campus police") employed by or contracted with the college or university to patrol the grounds and protect you (even from yourself!).
- What do they do?
  1. Respond to emergency calls, including reports of suspicious activities
  2. Act as an escort service, especially after dark or in lesser trafficked areas of campus
  3. Take criminal reports and work with local police to resolve situations quickly
  4. Conduct follow-up investigations on any 911 emergency and reports of theft, violence, or other abusive behavior, be it physical or substance
  5. During special events, monitor and maintain a proper flow of traffic at all times

Student Information Center

- What is it? The facility that usually serves as the hub of student activity, organized and unorganized.
- What can you find there?
  1. The main offices of most recognized student organizations and some social justice advocacy groups (e.g., NAACP)
  2. An eatery for light meals or quick snacks between classes
  3. A service desk offering work order request forms, fax or photocopy services, sports rental equipment, event registration, and various other resources or information
  4. Lounge furniture and a public television
  5. More and more often, wireless Internet service or a fee-based Internet café
  6. Maps or flyers for nearby supermarkets, shopping malls, sports arenas, movie theatres, and other cultural or entertainment centers

Student Healthcare Facility

- What is it? A basic medical facility provided by the college or university for the diagnosis and treatment of acute illnesses and minor injuries—a glorified version of your high-school's nurse's office.
- What services does it offer?
  1. Monitoring and treatment of chronic illnesses under the direction of your personal physician
  2. Routine immunizations for chicken pox, MMR, and TB, as well as polio, meningococcal, meningitis, and hepatitis A and B
  3. Routine, preventive gynecological care, including annual exams and pap smears
  4. Pain-free screenings for sexually transmitted diseases, including free anonymous HIV testing

5. Prescribed allergy injections under the administration of your allergist

6. Pharmacy services for prescriptions written by university health-care service providers

7. Information concerning good nutrition, regular exercise, and strategies for identifying or preventing common ailments

The process of discovering new boundaries really begins with the way you come to know your new surroundings. Academic advisement, the library, student center, campus security, and campus health-care facilities all fit into the learning cosmos of which you are a part. And once you learn your new backyard, seize regular opportunities to check out the neighborhood beyond. Go out with friends from class or your dorm, and as you share your past experiences, create new ones at the local diner or cinema as well as at museums, regional theatre productions, and concerts.

As you begin to feel your way around campus and community, start thinking outside them. Don't allow yourself to be boxed in by what has become familiar to you. God sent you to college to learn. Begin to stretch yourself. When you feel like you're living in the library, take time while you're there to read your way to Spain or Kenya. Learn to master Platonic philosophy the way Dr. Cornel West did. Reach beyond the heavens like Dr. Mae Jemison, the first African American female astronaut in space. Look at the nucleus of the cell like Dr. Edward Everett Just. Paint the world as Dr. Loïs Mailou Jones painted it. Then add to your own discourse.

I can't think of Rev. Dr. Martin Luther King Jr. delivering the "I Have a Dream" speech on the front steps of the Lincoln Memorial in 1963 without considering his early toiling with modern critical theory at Morehouse College. Nor can I think of Dr. Dorothy Height pushing back against the poverty of New York City in 1936 without first considering her significant wrestling with methods for community development and progressive social action at New York University. Learn to sharpen your God-given mind. Study hard. Discover new boundaries and discover yourself in the process.

Whether you live in a dorm, in an off-campus apartment, or commute by bus, car, or train, through *people, prayer,* and *patience,* you will come to know your new campus home—and what lies beyond it. *Prayer* will enable you to discern when to seek the services you need. *Patience* will give you the steadiness of heart to allow such services to make you a better student. *People* will give you the support you need as you step into new realities, boundaries, and new ways of thinking.

3

Establishing Good Study Habits

If you ever get the opportunity to watch a world class track-and-field meet, I advise that you go. Try to make it to the next Penn Relays at Franklin Field in Philadelphia, Pennsylvania. Pay close attention to how sprinters prepare themselves for their particular event. Usually, there will be some shimmying and shaking—to relax their muscles—as they approach the starting block. They'll discard all their outer garments, take their positions in their given lane, and prepare for the gun. If you notice, they carry nothing with them as they approach the block—just a focused mind, spiked shoes, and a streamlined track suit. They come prepared both physically and emotionally to compete in their given heat.

Much in the same way, if you're going to perform well in your academic studies at the college level, you'll need to come to your exams ultraprepared. Hear me out. I'm not asking you to shimmy and shake or do a spread-eagle stretch before you enter the classroom. However, much like the star track athlete approaching the starting block at the Penn Relays, you'll need to establish consistent habits that enable you to compete fairly while you're in college, and long after you enter into the real world.

Chances are you already are an above-average student. You would not be pursuing higher education if you weren't. But don't underestimate the weight of your academic load. Trust me. You'll need more than the "bling bling" to succeed in your undergraduate academic career. You'll need a focused and determined mind. *People, prayer,* and *patience* can help you in this endeavor.

Manage Your Time Effectively

- Always begin your time in a class lecture with a silent *prayer.* New information can make you as nervous as new people, and prayer will settle your nerves and focus your mind.

- When taking class notes, don't try to capture every word; concentrate on writing down all major dates, themes, and formulas. (For the technically advanced, use your laptop. Some versions even come with a voice recorder.)

- Review your notes one or two days after the date of the lecture. If you have any questions regarding a certain issue, ask your professor for clarity. A classmate might also be able to fill in a gap in your notes. Then, revisit your notes on the lecture once or twice over the upcoming weekend.

- Try to schedule three hours of private study for every hour of class time.

- Allow three weeks of intensive study when preparing for an exam date. Don't wait until the night before a scheduled exam to start cramming.

- Go to every class and be on time. Sit in the front of the classroom. It will be a signal that you have read your assignment. Professors know that those who sit in the back row do so because they haven't put the work in.

- Read between classes and during cancelled appointments. I've learned that most nuggets of wisdom are found when you stumble upon unexpected free time.

Manage Your Space Effectively

- Work in a quiet, well-lit area and avoid unnecessary distractions. Turn off 106 & Park. Ciara, 50 Cent, and Bow Wow will be there when you're finished.
- Bring a bottle of water and fresh fruit to your study area. Nuts, tofu, and soy products can provide nutrients your body needs to stay fresh and alert without the artificial highs of caffeine and sugar.
- Wear comfortable clothing when you study. If a pink Phat Farm sweat-suit works for you, then wear that. If a navy-blue pin-striped Brooks Brothers suit works for you, then wear that. Wear the attire that best helps you to feel successful in what you do.
- Make room for space between you and your study partners when you meet, and keep your stuff relevant to the task at hand. Don't clutter the table with other subjects or personal paraphernalia.
- Come to the study hall in a neat manner. I've seen too many study-groups break up because somebody didn't brush teeth or hit the showers before meeting the group.
- Organize your material. Use a desk, not a bed. Use folders, binders, stickies, highlighters, and colored pens to mark the information most crucial for you to remember. Use flash cards to aid memorization.
- Use flash drives and back-up discs to save data on your laptop. I once saw a student lose a 30-page document on his laptop the day the paper was due. He didn't have a backup copy—on disk or in hard copy. He hasn't been the same since.

Manage Your Friends Effectively

- Never spend more time socializing with friends than you do reading your texts.

- When it comes to study habits, spend your time with like-minded people. If you are serious about your academics, surround yourself with people who study the way you do.
- If you run across a problem you can't solve, share your concerns with your study partners. Good friends often talk through problems in plain conversation, making dense material easier for you to handle.
- When you become burned out with studying, take a break with your study partners or another friend. Go to a movie or the mall. Attend a game or a concert or visit a museum.
- Recognize when burnout gives way to fatigue. That's not the time for a study break with friends. Just retreat to your room or a quiet lounge and go to sleep. Even a 15-minute power nap can make a huge difference. You can't study well if you're fighting exhaustion.
- Most important, be honest with your friends. If you recognize a pattern of unpreparedness in your study partners, find out what's going on. They may be going through something. Or, maybe they no longer wish to maintain the same commitments they once made. If that is the case and if you've done all you can to inspire them, accept their wishes and move on. At all cost, you must maintain your A+ preparation for an A+ grade.

Let me give you an example of what it takes to earn an A+ grade. I can recall taking a course in African American history with Dr. Mia Bay, Associate Professor of History at Rutgers University. I read 150 pages a week in her class (yes, 150 pages—a week). I took extensive notes. I watched supportive documentaries, and then I visited Dr. Bay during her office hours to ask questions. I placed green and yellow stickies all over the refrigerator listing dates along with the names of special events and persons. Then I asked my study partners for their opinions on the topics discussed in class. I recorded their opinions and then doubled-back to the texts to determine whether their opinions were accurate or not. Then I shared my findings with them and the professor. Finally, for 14 days leading up to the midterm, I studied four hours a day, every day. I got an A on that test. Do you get the point? I don't claim brilliance per se, just a hard work ethic.

What if you find yourself at the end of the semester or, heaven forbid, at the end of freshman year and you're staring down a GPA of less than 3.25? Don't lose heart—but brace yourself because you have your work cut out for you. Consider a less demanding summer job, working 30 hours instead of 40+ a week, to allow yourself more time for getting a jump on next semester's reading. If the grade situation is really dire, look into taking a summer class to repair the damage. And talk to your academic advisor *now* about what strategies you'll need to put in place to recover lost ground. Don't hesitate to ask for help by talking to professors, taking advantage of peer tutors, or asking your friends and classmates for their support.

In closing, make sure you *pray* for wisdom when being introduced to new information. Concentrate on your subject matter. Read and read again. Be *patient*. The information and facts will come to your remembrance over time. Share your thoughts with your friends. Always hang around people who are smarter than you. Remember, *people* can help you work through obstacles. In all instances, you'll need to cultivate a focused and disciplined mind if you wish to succeed in your freshman year of college. Good study habits, discipline, and a will to strive for the A+ will increase your opportunity to earn the A+ on your exams.

For a quick meditation, here's a Scripture taken from 2 Timothy 2:15: "Study to shew thyself approved unto God, a workman that needeth not to be ashamed, rightly dividing the word of truth" (KJV).

4

Avoiding the Freshman Fifteen

Oh no! Oh no, no, no! Put the Häagen-Dazs ice cream down. I know. You have a critical writing essay paper due on Friday and a German quiz on Monday. You got a C on your first paper and you need to ace it to get the grade you want in the class. So, what will you do?

What do we usually do when we're in a jam and we need to hit a homerun to claim the victory? I'll tell you. We say good bye to the Ciara-like six pack and the Morris Chestnut "pecks." Sure we do. We crack open the computer, and while it's booting up, we call Dominoes Pizza for the daily special. Then we grab the Tostitos chips with the nacho cheese dip and the Snickers for dessert. Then what else? I'll tell you. Then we chug down the SoBe Adrenaline Rush soft drink or the Starbucks frappacino. And in extreme cases, we pour hot melted butter all over Top Ramen Oodles of Noodles. (Yeah, everybody eats Oodles of Noodles.)

If you ever look on the Internet, you'll find tons of websites dedicating their research and focus to the topic "The Freshman Fifteen." Can you guess what "fifteen" they're referring to? They're referring to the fifteen pounds of molten fat we tend to gain around the neck, waist, and thighs by the end of our freshman year. Do you know what the experts have figured out? When the pressure is on, we break down in our self-discipline and we consume junk. We tend to live off the chocolate chip brownie and French vanilla latte when we're in a jam.

I know what you're going to say: "I can't help it." Don't go there. In chapter 1, when I said you needed to connect with your friends and peers, I didn't mean you should eat your way to oblivion during every social interaction. Just because you have a mad midterm coming up and the study group is coming to your room for the final night of cramming, that doesn't mean you've earned your right to VIP status at the local Krispy Kreme. So please, fall back. Let's face it. If we're going to talk about being Christian in college, we might as well talk about what a healthy diet looks like. So, let's begin there. Let's talk about avoiding the "Freshman Fifteen."

Hocus-focus

If you are going to avoid the "Freshman Fifteen," first you must admit you *could* gain the "fifteen" if you aren't careful. I advise you to watch what you eat and when you eat it. Eat smaller portions. Avoid the foods heavy in fats, carbs, and sugars. Establish a self-enforced rule about no snacking after 8:00 p.m. There are no magic tricks to losing weight. Your schedule will become so crazy by midterms that if you aren't careful, you could find yourself eating raw hot dogs at three in the morning. So, don't eat unhealthy food at peculiar times in the day. Keep your focus. Stick to a regimented eating schedule.

Hydrate

I can't tell you enough: Drink a lot of H_2O. Hydrate yourself. While you're at it, buy stock in Dasani or Poland Spring. Have you noticed how the value of water has matured into a booming consumer market? Make sure you drink at least eight glasses of water a day. The water will flush your body of unnecessary impurities—and also help control the munchies.

Hit the Gym

Have you ever heard the comedian Martin Lawrence on reruns of "The Martin Lawrence Show"? He'd always say, "Get ta' stepping!" Well, you know what? I'm going to tell you the same thing: Get to stepping. Hit the gym! That's right. You don't need to commit to a $200 monthly membership fee at a local fitness to remain active. You can visit your campus gymnasium—I recommend going at least three times a week.

I started with 20 push-ups and sit-ups a day, and then walked a mile around the track. Maybe your school has stationary bikes or a pool. Males and females alike benefit from weight training. Many colleges and universities have trainers on staff who can offer suggestions for a personal exercise routine appropriate to your physical condition and fitness goals.

If you prefer the outdoors to the gym, get involved in hiking, cycling, or rock climbing. Pull out your inline skates and invite a friend to join you several mornings each week for a long cruise around the walkways of the campus. If you're a commuter, ride your bike, get off the bus a few stops early, or park in the farthest corner of the parking lot. In your daily comings and goings to class or meals, take the stairs instead of the elevator, or walk the long way around for the extra cardiovascular activity. Use your desk as if it were a Nautilus machine. Calf lifts and stomach crunches work well when you are fixed at one location for a long period of time. Simply constrict your muscles at one- or two-minute intervals and you will see amazing results.

The point is, you have to find ways to burn off excess calories now that you're away from whatever regular routine you might have had in the past and now that you're spending more and more hours sitting in class or at your desk. The key is to stay active and energized. Energy kills fat, and the endorphins produced by physical exertion are great for negating the effects of stress. Eating right will provide proper nutrition and assist you in making sound decisions as you navigate between colliding worlds.

Other Action Health Tips

- In the cafeteria, avoid fried foods or potent starches. Stay away from the foot-long hotdogs. Rebuke the nachos with cheese. A steak and cheese sub? No good. Pizza or pasta with sauce? In moderation. The carbohydrates in pasta and breads can short circuit your health and cause a buildup of body fat if you are not extremely active. I've found a large Caesar salad with grilled chicken to be just as satisfying as a plate of spaghetti with meatballs.

- Resist dessert except on special occasions. Give the ice cream sundae bar a pass, and try some yogurt sprinkled with granola instead. Exchange the fruit pie for a piece of fruit. A good banana or mandarin oranges provide for a stunning source of flavor and energy. And when your sweet tooth cannot be denied, indulge with discretion. Take the cake but skip the ice cream! "Cheat" with popcorn, but either pull out the old hot-air popper or get the plain microwave variety. If you must have flavoring, prefer light salt to butter and go with "light butter" rather than the "butter lover's"!

- Avoid microwaveable dinners. Instant macaroni and cheese will be the death of you. Even the "diet" versions microwave meals are lower in nutritional value than a fresh-cooked balanced meal. It is actually cheaper to purchase the individual ingredients for a week's worth of menus than to purchase a week's worth of prepackaged meals. You can find a convenient microwave cookbook in most bookstores that will teach you to prepare real meals with nearly the same ease that you can "nuke" a Hot Pocket or Lean Cuisine.

- Consider soy bean products as an alternative. The traditional high-protein food groups of meat and dairy also tend to be high in fat and cholesterol. Many companies offer soy-based alternatives that taste reasonably similar to the real thing. However, if you are a female with a history of estrogen-positive breast cancer, you should use such soy products in moderation and avoid concentrated sources of soy products at all costs. Courses in nutrition can help you in this endeavor.

- Find a liked-minded partner. This is another area where people can be a source of strength and encouragement. Identify a friend who will help hold you accountable in your new eating habits—and better yet, one who will join you in those habits! Invite a roommate or classmate to accompany you on your thrice-weekly trips to the gym or in your morning exercise routine. Avoid folks who will mock or undermine your commitment to cultivating healthy habits. The worst thing you can do is buddy up with someone who absolutely remains enslaved to the triple-decker with cheese. Pray for them—and keep stepping!

- Make sleep time sacred. Do not compromise on this. You cannot survive in college without maintaining good sleeping habits. Avoid the No-Doze or the high-caffeine energy drinks. Watch your consumption of sugar- and caffeine-laden soft drinks. Coffee and tea will ultimately fail you. Take sleeping seriously if you desire your body to replenish itself—and that means an average of eight hours a night. Consider it part of the biblical command concerning sabbath. Neglect it and you will find your performance decreasing by as much as 30 percent.

- Take a multivitamin. No matter what your age, your life as a student can be harsh. Moving from one classroom to the next with reading, research, and papers in between is taxing. Night classes are especially challenging. Multivitamins give your body the extra boost you need to sustain high levels of energy over longer periods of time. If you supplement a balanced diet with multivitamins in your daily routine, you will recognize a difference in the positive energy you exude.

- Paste or post Scripture all over your wall. With repetition, key Scriptures will come to change the way you view your body. If we would carefully consider how wonderfully we've been made, we would begin to visualize a more responsible manner by which we should live. For example, a great Scripture to meditate on is Romans 12:1, "Therefore, I urge you, brothers, in view of God's mercy, to offer your bodies as living sacrifices, holy and pleasing to God—this is your spiritual act of worship" (NIV).

5

Navigating a Collision of Worlds

I distinctly remember entering a dark holding area outside New York City's Hayden Planetarium Space Theater on the second floor. The Frederick Phineas and Sandra Priest Rose Center for Earth and Space housed a new and interesting exhibit entitled, "Cosmic Collisions." Within this digital display, spectators were launched through space and time to explore the spectacular evolution of our universe. As worlds collided into molten lava, our seats rattled. The digital display and accompanying sound affects were incredible. Trust me—X-Box 360's graphics had nothing on this exhibit. Have you ever played "Resistance: Fall of Man" on a surround sound system? Yeah . . . like that!

Why was the exhibit so important to me? In short, "Cosmic Collisions" sought to answer questions about the origins of our universe in the same way your freshman year offers suggestions for how best to pursue your purpose in life. It sought to make plain the fantastic idea you and I studied in high-school science: the Big Bang theory. Remember that? While the exhibit acknowledged the fact that our universe began "somehow," none of the exhibit's flashing lights and whirling novas gave credit to the God I believe initiated the process.

Even if you accept the Big Bang theory, you have to admit that God was in "the bang."

You ask, "And why is this an important observation to make?" Well, you and I really can't talk about successfully navigating through our own "collision of worlds" without first acknowledging the God who initiated our collegiate journey. While we're colliding with new theories, cultures, religious beliefs, and opportunities, we forget that God is the author of the freshman year through which we enter the thinking world. Here are a few action tips you can use to navigate the unfamiliar territory in the larger world you encounter during your freshman year.

Colliding Theories

It won't be only the Big Bang theory or Darwin's theory of evolution, which may collide with your traditional religious convictions about a seven-day Creation. It will be secular humanism and revisionist history and Fruedian psychology and feminist criticism and even Africentric scholarship—all offering different, sometimes competing perspectives on the world. Even within a single class, you'll feel disoriented bouncing between Plato, Aristotle, and Socrates, not to mention philosophers from Eastern or African cultures.

In this postmodern era, divergent perceptions of past, present, and future are the rule not the exception, and for many of us raised by a modernist generation that affirmed truth as a fixed construct, college is the first time we face the idea that truth may be, to a large extent, in the eye of the beholder. It can feel like a slippery slope, indeed, but don't fear! You always have solid ground to fall back on:

- Your faith. God is real, and God knows the answers, even when we do not. If you can hold on to those key truths, the Holy Spirit will help you navigate the rest.

- Your reason. God has given you a sound mind, so use it! Don't take anyone else's word for it. Search out the answers for yourself—and don't hesitate to ask others whom you trust and respect, even if you don't necessarily agree with them.
- Your experience. It is said that experience is the best teacher; hold on to that truism. No one can take away from you the weary years and silent tears that God has brought you through. What the Lord teaches you through those experiences, you can be sure of.
- God's Word. Last but far from least, you can cling to the Word of God in the Scriptures. True, your college experience may add to your knowledge and understanding of that Book and startle you with insights you had never imagined. But that's the best part about God's Word: It is living and breathing by the Spirit who quickens it in our hearts and lives.

Colliding Cultures

We have already talked about how important people are in our college experience, so don't be surprised if they are also part of the challenges you face. Many of us grew up in relatively tight-knit communities, where even if people didn't look just like us, they shared many of the same experiences—socially, economically, and experientially. College, especially if you go away to school or attend a large university, throws you into a much bigger pond!

You will meet people of different races, different socioeconomic backgrounds, different religions, who speak different languages or with different accents, who look at the world differently because the world from which they come is very different from yours. And when your different worlds collide in the new world of a college dorm, classroom, or cafeteria, you can expect some noise. Here are a few tips for filtering the cacophony of colliding cultures.

- Don't cover your ears or try to avoid the noise. Different doesn't mean dangerous or despicable. It's just different. Remember, to them, *you're* the one with the accent or the weird taste in food. Your face, style, and opinions are just as foreign to others as theirs are to you.
- Listen for common notes in the noise. Most of the time, you will discover that you have more in common than you have apart. Look for the familiar amid what seems foreign, and that should give you common ground to stand on.
- Try to create new harmonies. Meeting new people and trying new things is one of the greatest opportunities college offers you. Take advantage of it! Ask questions with respect and real interest; answer questions without defensiveness or impatience. Learn everything you can from the new cultures and people you encounter.

Colliding Beliefs

College may offer you your first introduction to people who share your passionate beliefs—in something completely different. It won't just be your first encounter with a Jew or Muslim or Hindu. It may be your first real conversation with a Mormon or Jehovah's Witness, with a Catholic or Pentecostal Christian, with a Seventh-day Adventist or a Unitarian Universalist. It may even be a surprising debate with an Episcopalian or a Baptist (of one kind or another!).

Colliding with the sincere but divergent beliefs of others, especially people whom you come to know and care about, can be disturbing and disorienting. I offer the following action steps for navigating this particular collision of worlds.

- Talk about it. As suggested earlier, ask questions about other faiths—and do so respectfully, with a genuine interest in hearing the answer. Share your own beliefs with confidence but not arrogance. Conversation, not conversion, discussion, not debate, should be the goal for such interactions.

- Read about it. Explore the scriptures and other writings of the other faith. Compare them with your own Bible and denominational teachings. Don't just read James Cone and Katie Cannon. Read Ghandi and Lao Tsu to understand more fully how others think about God and life. What do your beliefs have in common, and where do you part ways?
- Pray about it. Of course, differences in religious beliefs weigh more heavily on us than differences in culture or academic theory. For many people, eternity is at stake when you talk about God, the human condition, and life after death. So, ask God to open doors of opportunity to share your experiences and beliefs—and then trust the Holy Spirit to do the rest. After all, even the most zealous evangelist must concede: we don't save anyone. Jesus does!

No matter what collisions of theory, culture, and belief you may face, keep in mind that God created the world—all of it! And even as the Lord started you on your college journey, God will also help you navigate the twists and turns along the way. So take these final words of exhortation with you as you fix your eyes on the finish line of your freshman year.

- Be courageous. You are a descendent of thoughtful and courageous people. Think about the great students who came before you. Mary McLeod Bethune would walk miles to school just to engage in a daily collision of new ideas. Bethune's courage to learn positioned her to receive college scholarships, and eventually in 1904, she opened what we now know as Bethune-Cookman College.
- Be smart. Prepare yourself for the collisions to come by establishing first who you are and what you believe. Then open yourself to learn what God desires to teach you. Christopher Gardner

(recently portrayed by actor Will Smith in the film *The Pursuit of Happyness*) is a self-made millionaire who endured poverty and homelessness to become one of the most influential brokers on Wall Street. Why did Christopher Gardner, an African American male and single father, succeed? Gardner credits his mother's courage, but I would add that Gardner demonstrated the intelligence needed to act when opportunity presented itself. Be smart.

• Be humble. Not only in relation to a sovereign God, but also to other people. Jesus may have said that he is the Way, Truth, and Life, but no one of us is. Be humble enough to learn from others and to look for new insights into God and the world through other people's experiences. Even the great patriarch Moses didn't know how to use what was in his hand until God showed him (see Exodus 4:1-5). We all need to encounter new people and ideas to help us see what we could not see on our own. Humility will allow us to set aside our own perspective for the sake of respecting the views of others.

As you enter into your sophomore year, remember to be courageous, smart, and humble. Meditate on Joshua 1:8. And keep in mind you could not have made it on your own. Holding on to *people*, *prayer*, and *patience* has enabled you to make it when you thought you couldn't. Celebrate this accomplishment, and yet remain disciplined in your habits and in your thought-life. You've finished only one leg of the journey. There is much more we need to tend to in the second year.

SOPHOMORE YEAR

Getting Serious

6

Choosing a Companion

Wow! Welcome back on campus. You made it through the summer. You earned a little money with a summer job. You made a few connections through an internship with Ford or Pfizer. You even changed your hairstyle a little bit. Last year you made it through school with one pair of sneakers and two pairs of shoes. This year you've got the Mello's in sky blue, the King James in green and white, and the alligator Air Force One's in red, blue, and white. You've got the Nine West "Paskel" Bootie, the Air Max 360, and the new Prada round toe. Wow! Not only am I feeling you; everybody on campus is feeling you too. If there's one thing you can expect to experience by your sophomore year of college, it will be an opportunity to test the dating pool. Mark my words. If someone hasn't already done so, somebody is going to attract your eye, and whether you are asked or do the asking yourself, you're going to want to explore a romantic relationship in this new world called college.

Choosing Your Future First

Love can show up anywhere. It can show up behind the lunch counter, in the library, or at the basketball game. And exploring new relationships is always good. God intended that you have a good time while in college, and that includes some healthy romance in addition to all the other friendships you will form.

But I have to be honest with you, and I need to say this before we get into the do's and don'ts of Christian dating. You came to school to get an education, so you really have to use caution when you date. I'm serious. I know the images on TV and in the movies suggest that having a romance while in college is a big deal. And it is. But the truth of the matter remains: you're laying out a lot of paper for a college education and your focus needs to be on developing life skills that will equip you to change and transform your community. Don't blow this opportunity to become great. Have fun, keep things light, but also keep things in perspective. Stay the course. You've got work to do.

Choosing Your Companion Second

If you do end up connecting yourself to that special someone in the chemistry lab or in art history class, let me at least help you in the matter. Choosing a special companion or friend while in college will require *integrity, introspection,* and *insight*. Don't get caught up with the "grill in his mouth" or the dimensions of her figure. Even when romance isn't involved, you need Jesus Christ in your life to help you determine which friends are best for you. The Lord is even more important when you are considering an intimate companion!

Sometimes an acquaintance may appear in your life for a short season—someone you enjoy hanging out with on the weekends or with whom you may attend a special event. But do not confuse such acquaintances with the one whom God will call to be in your life for the long haul. Here are a few tips you can follow when trying to discern the difference between Mr./Ms. Right and Mr./Ms. Right Now.

Integrity

- Establish reasonable boundaries. If you give out your number to the hottie you met in the grocery store, don't accept phone calls before 9:00 a.m. or after 9:00 p.m. If your acquaintance consistently violates these simple boundaries, leave that relationship alone. You have work to do, and friends of all sorts need to give you space to get that work done.

- Don't follow the crowd, figuratively or literally. Don't compromise your Christian convictions just because your acquaintance offers you a drink or a hit. Don't neglect your academic priorities to accept an invitation to stay out late when you ought to be studying for tomorrow's big test. Don't agree to go somewhere or do something that makes you uncomfortable just because everyone else (including that special friend you're hoping to attract) is taking part.

- Always look to meet your special acquaintance in open space and with at least two other friends. You know the Scripture, "Where two or three are gathered in my name"? Heed what Jesus Christ was suggesting. You should always want the presence of the Lord to be readily accessible while dating. Having at least two other trustworthy friends with you will ensure your protection from peculiar behavior.

- Keep your clothes on. Never allow your acquaintance to see you exposed. Your body belongs to God. Many would suggest college is the best place to explore your sexuality. Wrong. No sex until marriage. When on a date, wear clothes that are comfortable, but not too provocative. Scale back on the pierced tongue action. Avoid situations where you could be pressured—or tempted to put on the pressure yourself. As the saying goes, "If you don't start none, there won't be none."

Introspection

- Trust your instincts. Remember the instructions of your parents and pastor. Recall the wisdom of your athletic coach or your grandmother. Expect yourself to be treated as if you were royalty. If you see signs of profanity, deceit, or physical abuse, you are spending time with the wrong person. Walk away!

- Ask for help. Sometimes a relationship will go sour on you. Don't lie to yourself and try to deny that you've found yourself in a harmful situation. If you are being manipulated or coerced emotionally, break it off and confide in a friend who will keep you accountable. If you are being harassed, stalked, or sexually or physically abused, call campus security and report it to the police. Tell your RA, the police, a medical professional, a counselor, and a friend. Call your family—the ones you trust the most. They are always poised and ready to handle your business when you need them to.

- Never settle for less. Most of us desire to meet someone who holds to the same standards that have been ingrained in us. Do not settle. If the relationship is causing you to compromise who you are in Jesus Christ, break it off. And just because you broke it off does not mean you need to avoid your ex-acquaintance. Go to class. Be respectful. And stay connected to mutual friends who respect you. But always remain true to yourself.

Insight

- Look for a reflection of God's image. "No one has ever seen God; if we love one another, God lives in us, and his love is perfected in us" (1 John 4:12, NRSV). True courtship will enable you to learn more about God and more about who you are in Jesus Christ. If you don't see Jesus in the relationship, leave it alone.

- Pay attention to details. Where did you meet your friend? How do you most often spend time together? What do you talk about? The answers to these and similar questions can reveal a lot. If you met at a drinking party, spend most of your time swapping spit, and rarely talk unless it's to gossip about other people, you might reconsider your choice of companions—and why you were willing to accept such a relationship in the first place.
- Judge a tree by its fruit. If you see reckless behavior, take note of it. If the humor is always sarcastic or mean-spirited, ask yourself why. If the attention you get is obsessive or negligent, question that too. Observe how he or she treats other people—including professors, strangers, children, the elderly, and even family members. What behaviors are the exception and which are the rule? Actions really do speak far louder (and more accurately) than words.

I must conclude by reiterating what I said at the start of this chapter. You came to college to learn. Stay focused. Study hard. If you find yourself paying more attention to your special friend than to your school work, you will flunk out. Trust me when I tell you that the quickest way to lose a college sweetheart is to flunk out of college. Handle your business because once your education gets derailed, getting back on track will cost you time, money, and probably a good share of pride.

Choosing the right companion takes hard work. You'll need *integrity, introspection,* and *insight* to help you survive the temptations that come your way. In the next chapter we'll deal with these temptations in greater detail. At least now you have a working foundation from which we can develop a deeper conversation. So, let's get deep.

7

Resisting Temptation

The Gospel of Matthew offers a clear example of what temptation seeks to accomplish in your life. Temptation seeks to test, try, and entice you to do evil, plain and simple. In Matthew 4:1-11 Satan attempts to divert Jesus from God's way of accomplishing his mission. You will find throughout your college career that people, places, and players will seek to do the same to you. There will be moments when someone asks you to do something contrary to what you believe. There will be times when you yourself will want to do something you know you shouldn't do. Can we keep it real? If you are going to make it in college, you'll need to learn how to say no to the tempter as well as to the temptation.

So let's dialogue on some critical do's and don'ts of Christian living so that we can remain whole throughout our Christian journey on campus. Let's talk about how you can stay *honest, holy*, and *humble* during your college years.

Stay Honest

- No lying. If you failed the test because you didn't study, just say so. Don't lie to your parents, pastor, and friends when explaining why you underachieved. There will always be another day when you can redeem yourself. Also, resist the temptation to lie to your special friend. If you want to go out on a date with someone else, tell the truth. Don't be ashamed. And don't get caught out there. Lying will destroy the strongest of relationships. I lost a very good friend in undergraduate school over a lil' lie that I told.

- No plagiarizing. Do not succumb to the pressure of using other people's ideas when you write college papers. That includes the ideas you may not quote verbatim but that you paraphrase in your own words! If you get an idea from an outside source, cite the source from which the idea emerged. By any other name, plagiarism is cheating. Resist the temptation to cut the corners of your research when you are under the gun. One of the worst things that can happen to you is to get expelled from school because you cheated.

Stay Holy

- No sex. I can't say this enough: Practice celibacy. Sex outside of marriage kills relationships and it kills careers. With the rising incidence of HIV/AIDS and other sexually transmitted diseases, sex can even kill *you*. While statistics suggest our generation is 25 percent more sexually active than any previous generation, remember that as the saints of God we have been called to live the celibate life until marriage. One way to guard yourself against this temptation is to be careful about what you listen to on the radio and what you view on TV. The booty-shake isn't for you, and you shouldn't expect to see that kind of conduct being displayed by your friends and special acquaintances.
- No sleepovers. If you creep with it, you'll sleep with it, so stay above reproach. If you live off campus, please do not invite anybody of the opposite sex to spend the night with you. If you are

studying in your room late at night, don't slip into anything provocative in the name of "getting comfortable." And when you are entertaining a special friend, resist the temptation to prolong casual visitations past 8:00 p.m. Yes, I said 8:00 p.m.! The later it gets, the more vulnerable and susceptible you will be to physical temptation. Your mind will tell you no, but your body will tell you yes.

- No nasty blogs. The quickest way to play yourself is to post nasty or pornographic blog messages on the Internet. Trust me—people talk. Somebody will find your posting and tell your special friend. You will be over before you even get started. Avoid the temptation of trying to look overly sexual on the Internet. There are predators out there, and they will show up at your campus dorm room.

- No drugs. Part of staying holy involves staying clean. And that may be more difficult than "just say no." If you *must* go to the frat party, don't drink the punch! I can remember my first week on campus drinking "blue punch." (Sorry, Sigmas!) It was a Friday night and I didn't wake up until Sunday morning. Watch those students who have a rep for spiking the drinks at every party. Watch for yourself and watch for your friends. I can't tell you how many cases have been reported of date-rape because someone slipped "a lil' extra flava" in the party punch.

Stay Humble

- No competition. Oh yes, this is a good one! Please do not try to keep up with everybody and everything that you see. Your Sunday school teacher would call this "coveting" or "idolatry." Remember those words? There will always be someone on campus who has more money than you, more charisma than you, and more friends than you. So what? Don't try to be anything more than who

40

you are in Jesus Christ. Be yourself. Resist the temptation to try to compete with your classmates.

- No fronting. I can remember putting socks in the bottom of my sneakers because I wanted to be taller than 6'2" when I competed on the basketball court. You know what? My sneakers came off during a lay-up and black dress socks sprang out of the souls of my shoes onto the court. Do you want to talk about embarrassment? Please do not play yourself. God made you as you are. Be proud of who God created you to be.

- No fighting. This is a hard one, but I have to say it. Please resist this temptation to fight with folks. Maintain your cool. Keep the peace. If somebody offends you, just walk away and leave the rest to God. I know this sounds corny, but God really has your back. If you get caught fighting, you will be expelled. I can remember entering into a physical confrontation with someone during my freshman year. I escaped getting expelled, but my college sweetheart saw a side of me I never wanted her to see—and I still regret that I never said I was sorry. Take it from me—fighting wounds the flesh and it wounds the soul.

You see, temptations can come from many different angles and many different places. If you want to follow Jesus, do what Jesus did in Matthew 4. Jesus answered every temptation with the Word of God. Read your Bible daily. Why? The more you read the Bible, the more you'll understand who God created you to be. The more you understand who God created you to be, the more you'll want to become that person. Are you following the logic here? The Word of God will give you the courage to say no to every situation that challenges your identity in Jesus Christ. Stay *honest, holy,* and *humble,* and keep your eyes on God, who will never lead you into temptation.

8

Picking Your Major

I can recall producing a record for Shaquille O'Neil entitled "You Can't Stop the Reign" featuring the Notorious B.I.G. (Yeah, me. I produced that record. And it's a long story.) In any case, as I settled myself in Shaq's house in Orlando, Florida, and I'm telling you it was huge, I noticed something about Shaq that really impressed me. Shaq had every minute of his day calculated and accounted for. Shaq was either in the weight room, the studio, the gym, or with his family. Every single day Shaq followed the same routine. And you know what? It was obvious Shaq loved what he did for a living. Shaq loved to play basketball, and he loved to work on his game. Much in the same way, you'll need to follow your own passion when you choose your college major. Choose a major because you love the vocational field. Just like Shaq, play the game because you love the game.

Choosing the Right Path

In choosing your major for college, you are expressing who you believe God has called you to be. Is this process easy? Of course not!

In fact, most students will change their major twice before they graduate. That's *at least* twice. So, you shouldn't panic in the beginning of your college journey if you haven't yet understood fully who God has called you to be.

If I can offer any advice to a Christian in college it would be this: Trust God. Is that advice simple enough for you? Trust God. God will order your steps in choosing the road you should take. When we put our trust in God, God helps us to choose the right path.

Questions from the Past

Take a moment to consider the first 12 to 18 years of your life—before you started thinking about income brackets or fast cars or luxury homes. If you are returning to college later in life, think about the years before your first career, before marriage and children made a job a means to an end instead of the fulfillment of a vocational dream. Then ask yourself these kinds of questions:

- What things in life interested me as a child, and how did God play a part in revealing those interests to me?
- What clubs and associations did I find myself in?
- Which subjects of study were most meaningful for me in high school? Which subjects was I most successful in?
- What persons in my past were most inspiring? Whose accomplishments did I find myself wanting to imitate—a family member, teacher, mentor, friend, or stranger?
- What kind of volunteer work did I do? What parts of it did I enjoy?
- What types of jobs or professional careers appealed to my imagination and why?
- Most important, what declarations did a pastor or trusted faith leader make over my life?

Questions for the Present

Now think about your life today and consider it from all angles. What insights do your current experiences give you into your character, your gifts, and your divine calling? Ask yourself:

- How am I being affirmed—in what areas and by whom?
- Do I prefer mathematics or science to history or literature courses?
- Am I generally introverted or extroverted? Does my energy come from being alone or from being with other people?
- What passions have other people identified in my life and encouraged me to pursue?
- In my summer job or first career, how has my job description shaped the way I see myself?
- What hereditary gifts and talents do I recognize in myself? How do I take after my mother, father, grandparent, or another family member?
- What special abilities in my repertoire demand further refinement?

These questions seek to identify your current strengths and interests as clues to a vocational calling. If you excel in writing or speaking, consider the field of communications. Do you sense a call to fulltime ministry? I recommend religious studies as a possible major. Do you love to sing or dance? A fine arts major such as theater or music may be a consideration. Perhaps you desire to ascend to the Supreme Court or become a voice in the legislature, be it local, state, or national. Consider a major in prelaw.

Questions for the Future

Finally, you need to look beyond today and even tomorrow or next week. Think about the big picture and where you would like to be in five, ten, or 25 years. Ask yourself these questions:

44

- What matters most in my life?
- How do I envision myself contributing to society?
- Do I desire to remain in one particular vocation for 30 years, or would I prefer a career path that leads me from one step to another?
- What other priorities will I want to pursue, in addition to career or vocational goals?
- What is my timeline for preparation? Will I need four years or 12 to ready myself for my preferred vocation? (If you can barely tolerate your hours in the classroom and dread the thought of two more years of undergrad schooling, you might reconsider a plan to pursue a prolonged career in education!)

Do Your Homework

If I know God at all, the Holy Spirit has probably provided answers to most of these kinds of questions already. You probably already know whether you prefer working with people to sitting alone with a computer—or if you crave time outdoors over being confined to a desk. If you don't already know your ministry gifts, ask your pastor to recommend an assessment tool—there are many—and be sure to solicit insights from those who know you best. They will probably just confirm what you already know in your spirit.

Once you have done your homework relating to yourself, do some research about the career options that seem well matched to someone with your gifts and abilities. Find out what academic major is recommended for people interested in that vocation. And be sure to consult the appropriate periodicals that project whether a particular occupation will become obsolete in the next few years. Read *Black Enterprise, The Economist,* and the *Journal of Accountancy.* Check AllBusiness.com. All four are great resources. Check for growth rates in your particular field of interest. I've heard that certain fast-food chains will begin to outsource their drive-through order-taker positions. Can you imagine placing an order for fries with someone in another city or country? I imagine that soon our fast-food chains will become completely automated. What's the point? We can never assume what we see today will exist in our tomorrow. So speak to the experts. Think critically about the future before you choose your college major.

Action Steps for Choosing the Right Major

- Thoroughly investigate your college's course catalogue. They not only offer basic descriptions of your program options, but they will outline exactly what preparation you need to complete the specialized major or honors program you seek.
- Connect with your academic advisor. Tell your advisor the desires of your heart. Do not hide behind a mask of indifference or deny your dream because of shame or insecurity. If you really want to major in premed, confess that desire and let your advisor direct you in the necessary steps to achieve that dream.
- Talk to your professors. Many professors are experts in their field, and you want their support and insight. If you want to be a chemist, ask your chemistry professor about his or her willingness to supervise your labs. If not, the quality of your lab training could be compromised.
- Talk to your college alumni office. Often alumni possess valuable connections that may help you secure internships or jobs. Based on their experiences, they will tell you whether your expectations are realistic or not.
- Do not allow *MTV Cribs* or *Pimp My Ride* or anything else in the media to influence the decisions that you make. Remember, you are seeking to do the will of God, reconciling the world unto God

through your vocational service. Do not allow shallow ambitions to misguide you.

- Start looking now for internships or summer job opportunities that test the answers you have begun to formulate to the questions about your past, present, and future. Search monstertrak .monster.com or Internjob.com. These search engines will help you find the internships you want. Believe me—the best way to discern the career track that's right for you is to test the waters. Even an unpaid internship will ultimately be money in your pocket—not only for the valuable experience it contributes to your résumé but also for the tuition and time it may save you when you discover you really weren't cut out for the profession you were aiming for.

- Most important of all, pray. Ask God to give you wisdom as you decide which college major works best for you. Do not panic. Do not be afraid. Trust that God is in control and God will give you the peace and comfort you need as you make your decision.

9

Getting Enough Sleep

Until this day I cringe when I hear the underground hip-hop classic "One on One," featuring Nasty Nas and Craig Live on the movie soundtrack *Street Fighter*. Why do I cringe? I cringe because I produced the song. Yeah, I produced that song, too. It's true. One evening Nas and I were in the Greene St. Recording Studio in New York City with a group of corporate executives, and we had only nine hours to cut the song or it wouldn't make the soundtrack. Needless to say, we didn't get any sleep that night, and I'm not so sure I gave Nas the best I had as a producer. I was tired and I wanted to go home.

Our culture has become so task-oriented that we assume we don't need sleep anymore to perform our particular functions on any given day. We all buy into that con at one point or another. When we're young, we figure that because of our youth we don't need a lot of rest to do the things we do. When we're more mature in age, we assume that our ambitious drive will compensate for an obvious lack of sleep. In both cases we are sadly mistaken.

If you desire to achieve optimum success in your undergraduate studies, you'll need to get the sleep required to reach the lofty goals you've set for yourself. How will you become the next Toni Morrison, an African American winner of the Nobel Prize for Literature, if you can't stay awake? It won't happen.

The National Sleep Foundation has long recommended eight hours of sleep per night. The benefits are obvious—and the consequences of neglecting adequate rest are far-reaching. In fact, the December 11, 2003, issue of *Harvard Gazette* reported that not only were Harvard students getting insufficient sleep, but the lack was affecting their physical health and their academic performance.[1] If you're like those students at Harvard, you probably skimp on sleep during the week and try to "catch up" on the weekends by sleeping in late. The experts call that "sleep bulimia" because it imitates the binge/purge cycle of the eating disorder—and they observe that the physical effects are almost as harmful.

Action Steps for Getting Enough Sleep

Obviously, college life puts more demands on your time. In addition to classes and study time, you also want time for socializing and engaging in extracurricular activities. Carving out time for sleep may seem impossible. Here are a few practical suggestions to help you find some balance in your sleep life.

- Maintain a regular sleep schedule, avoiding deprivation during the week and sleeping until noon on the weekend. On any given night, allot yourself *at least* seven hours of sleep—and whenever possible, make it the recommended eight!

- Give your body time to adjust to your new class schedule. If you have an early morning class this semester, practice going to sleep an hour earlier the night before for two weeks prior to the start of the semester. (I learned this trick from a teammate years ago.)

- Know your inner-time clock. You psychology majors out there call this our "circadian pacemaker." My friends will tell you—I cannot study late into the evening. My inner-time clock—my circadian pacemaker—produces the most energy early in the day. By 4:00 p.m. I'm usually *finito*. Get to know your own "pacemaker" and schedule your days accordingly.

- Don't take over-the-counter medications to stay awake. They may seem like a good idea the night before your big exam, but take it from someone who knows. You'll feel horrible when it wears off, and it's hard to recall the information you studied all night when you have a No-Doz hangover.
- Don't rely on caffeine or other energy boosters to get you through that early class or late-night study session. Stay away from the coffee. Skip the Red Bull. Watch your soft-drink intake. Caffeine dissolves the body chemical called adenosine. Without it our body cannot relax to enjoy an uninhibited resting period. So long after you're ready to crash, that late-night latte is going to keep your brain and body humming.
- Build a nap time into your daily routine. Instead of spending that free hour on the phone or on the Nintendo, go to sleep. I promise, you will feel much better about yourself, especially when you need to write a paper that is due.
- Even if your schedule *doesn't* allow it, take the nap you need. Research specialists suggest even if you don't suffer from sleep deprivation now, the development of bad sleeping habits while in college often lead to sleep deprivation later. Even a 15- or 20-minute "power nap" can revitalize you for the next few hours.
- Get enough exercise. Physical activity doesn't just help keep off that Freshman (or Sophomore) Fifteen. When you exercise, you stimulate your blood flow, you generate "feel-good" endorphins, and you force your body to rest better later in the day.
- Use an alarm clock. When I use an alarm clock I never worry about getting up on time. This alleviates any anxiety caused from a fear

of oversleeping through a morning class. Also, I recommend turning the clock away from you after you set the time. This keeps you from looking at the time all night long, further preventing you from getting a good night sleep.

• If you struggle with getting up in the morning, put your alarm clock across the room. That way you can't reach out and hit "snooze" without ever lifting your head from the pillow. You might also consider using a bright light to shake off the cobwebs. Don't stumble around in the dark, thinking the absence of stimuli will let you wake up more "gently." Get up and turn on the lights to jolt your body awake when the time comes.

A Good Rest = A Better Grade

Remember, you spend a lot of energy in the classroom trying to retain information, and many students add commuting hours to the equation, not to mention the study sessions and reading assignments. It shouldn't be surprising that the stress of college produces depression in many students—and a classic symptom of depression is a desire to sleep.

In such circumstances, it's tempting to take a pill like No-Doz or spend a small fortune on Starbucks or Red Bull. Some students will even succumb to the temptation of even stronger supplements—illegal ones. It's understandable. After all, you want to live up to the expectations of others. You've been told all your life that you have the determination of a Sojourner Truth, who brought innumerable slaves to freedom via the Underground Railroad. Family, friends, and mentors expect you to equal the brilliance and achievements of an Alan Shaw, brilliant innovator of new software systems.

But I have to be honest with you. Your attempts to keep yourself alert using caffeine, No-Doz, and other artificial energy boosters will fail you. You risk losing the information you fought so hard to retain when you use such methods. Nothing can replace the quality of a well rested body and a sleep-recharged brain.

I once pulled a double all-nighter, staying awake for two days to study for a big exam. I figured that if I read over all the material a certain number of times, even at the cost of getting no sleep, I would have a better chance at recalling the data. Guess what happened? I performed miserably. I could not remember any of the information I needed. My short-term memory had been shot, and that meant I had to work that much harder on the final to get a decent grade. Please do not follow in my footsteps. Take your time. Pace yourself. Balance your days and nights, and get the sleep that you need. Eight hours of good sleep each night along with a good library schedule and a good study group will almost always guarantee a good grade on an exam.

Note

1. Beth Potier, "Go to bed! say experts at pajama party panel," *Harvard Gazette* (December 11, 2003). http://www.news.harvard.edu/gazette/2003/12.11/03-sleep.html (accessed March 14, 2007).

10

Forsaking Not the Tabernacle

OK, now we've reached one of the most important chapters in this book. Earlier I suggested that you should trust God in everything that you do. When we put God first, God has promised to order our steps along the road. When we put our trust in God, God helps us to choose the right path. And while that trust is critical, we can't just stop there. Yes, we need to trust in God's provision and guidance, but we also need to confess God's goodness. We need to thank God continuously for what God has done. Give God praise for what God has already done in your life—in these first two years of college!

How do I propose that we thank God for these miraculous works? By going to church to worship! Yes, I said it. I said *go to church!* 50 Cent and Young Jeezy can't help you with your soul. BET's College Hill and 106 & Park can't save you from the toils of life. But you know what? Jesus can. If we're going to talk about being both Christian and successful while in college, we cannot forsake the tabernacle of God. We've gotta take it to church.

You Need the Church

You might question the importance of today's African American student going to church while in college. Why should you go to church? Well, the answer is quite simple. You need God, and connecting with the Body of Christ on earth will help you maintain your connection to the Lord.

The benefits to you are numerous. A strong Bible-based church will equip you with the scriptural wisdom you need to you make the transition from adolescence into spiritual adulthood. A warm congregation will provide a loving touch and a helping hand to those of us who are away from home and need the love of the Lord. A good shepherd-pastor will nurture us and encourage us to embrace our greatness, especially in those moments when we think we're more sinner than sanctified. It is within the church where we find the love of God. And when we experience the love of God being active and present in our life, we will find our purpose for living.

The Church Needs You

Yes, the church needs you as well. Christ's Body needs your gifts to act as an arm of service or hand of compassion, as the feet bringing Good News or the eyes perceiving injustice. What's more, churches in contemporary times often lack the presence of dynamic and youthful people—and "youthful" isn't just an age thing. No matter your chronological age, as a college student, you can provide an infusion of youthful energy that other age groups will feed on.

Think about it. You're learning something new every day; each class introduces you to new people, new ideas, and new experiences. Your presence in a congregation expands the horizons of that church, even as your own horizons broaden.

It isn't only what you bring to the church. It is also who you are. You are an educated black man or woman. You are going places and doing things with your life. You have a dream, a vision, a plan, and you are pursuing it. The church today needs people like you to act as role models for the next generation. Parents want their daughters to hang around with someone who is studying premed at John Hopkins and their sons spending time with someone who is a religious studies major at Morehouse or Fisk. Your time may be constrained by your commitment to school, but you can still offer the gift of service to a church to make that local body of believers a bit stronger.

Finding a Church That Is Right for You

If you are a commuter, living at home and attending a local college or university, this may just mean continuing regular attendance at your home church. Your class schedule and coursework may require you to scale back on some of your ministry commitments, of course. Clearly, you won't be able to attend every midweek prayer service or Bible study when you have evening classes or major papers due. But I'm talking about maintaining a foundational connection to the Body of Christ during your college experience.

For the student who is attending a college or university away from home, or even for the young person who is developing a faith that is independent of your parents or grandparents, your task will be a little more challenging.

Ask Around

The first step I would recommend is to ask around. Ask the college chaplain for a list of local congregations; the chaplain may even have a recommendation based on your stated preference for a particular denomination, congregational size, or worship style. Then poll your Christian friends, especially those who live locally or have been on campus longer, and find out which churches best serve the needs of the young adult population. "Where can I get a word from the Lord?" is the question you need to ask somebody.

Get a Feel for It

Visit a few churches, and then when you identify one that seems most right, go back a few times to get a feel for it. Attend three or four services before you make any decision. I've learned from experience that often a visiting speaker or major celebration or tragedy in the life of the congregation can throw off a church's usual calendar and routine. Don't judge the flavor of a church based on a single service; the menu may have changed due to unforeseen or unusual circumstances. Allow yourself to experience the church over time and, if possible, in several different settings—Sunday morning worship, Wednesday night Bible study, and this Saturday's annual church picnic. After all, a church is more than a worship service; it is a community of people. You'll need a little time to see how the members interact with one another and with you!

Identify the Vision of the House

Read the vision statement of the church. Many churches print this in their weekly bulletin or post it prominently in the sanctuary or fellowship space. If you can't find it, ask an usher or another member of the church leadership. (If the vision statement is not readily and publicly available, what does that say about the congregation and its leadership?)

You will also want to know about the church's statement of beliefs. Does it believe in the Trinity? Will the church support women in leadership? What baptism does the church practice? What is the congregation's priority in ministry—evangelism, discipleship, service, justice? How do the church's beliefs compare with your own?

If you are a traditional college student (i.e., age 18–23), I strongly recommend finding out about the congregation's young adult ministry. Are there youth leaders in place who share in the overall leadership of the church? How many other college students or young people your age attend that church? If the church is close to the college campus but has no presence on the campus grounds, how equipped will the leaders and members be in addressing your needs as a young college student?

Get to Know the Heart of the Shepherd

Find time to meet the pastor, and be prayerful about that meeting. Ask God to help you discern the heart of this undershepherd. Assess the pastor's theology, character, and relationship with the members of the church. Will he or she challenge you in your own spiritual growth? Would you feel comfortable with this pastor's involvement in your life?

The traditional college student should also determine if the pastor likes young people. Some leaders don't! They look at teens and 20-somethings as suspect or fail to take them seriously. So, look for a pastor who does care about young people and whose church offers outstanding college and young adult ministries. You'll want to find out if there is a youth or young adult pastor on staff. If so, what role would such a person play in your spiritual development?

When I served as the first-ever minister of youth to the Bronx Christian Fellowship where the Rev. Dr. Suzan Johnson Cook is the senior pastor, I made sure that my youth were in school, in the books, in the bank, and in the church. I charged the youth to excel because Jesus Christ charged me to excel. Make sure your youth leader has the heart of your senior shepherd. And make sure your senior shepherd has the heart of Jesus Christ.

When to Join

Take your time. Don't grab the hand of fellowship at the first church you visit or on your first visit. Work your way through the process outlined above, and only then, if you feel the Spirit's leading, go forward to make the commitment to the local Body of Christ.

Many churches offer college students "watch-care" status, in which you serve as a member while you are in school. These types of churches are a blessing in that they don't seek to blot your membership in your home church. They only desire to provide spiritual support and nurturing while you remain fixed within their jurisdiction of influence during college.

Putting Faith to Action

Once you have joined a church, find a way to become active there. Remember, you want to offer God thanks for providing a way out of no way. God put you in college. The least you can do is find a way to serve a local Body of Christ while you are there—out of gratitude for what God has done. (If you do not feel a compulsion to thank God in worship and service, I would get my spiritual heart checked out. You may need the church more than you realize!)

Whether at home or away during your college years, you *will* be tempted to forego Sunday morning worship when you have reading to do and papers to write and exams coming up. You could use those hours to sleep or study or even catch up on laundry! But remember Scripture's exhortation in Hebrews 10:24-25: "And let us consider how to provoke one another to love and good deeds, not neglecting to meet together, as is the habit of some, but encouraging one another, and all the more as you see the Day approaching" (NRSV).

JUNIOR YEAR

Getting Ahead

11

Connecting in Community

While attending the 2006 NAACP Leadership 500 Summit in Destin, Florida, I entered into what I consider to be one of the most privileged conversations I've had in a long time. I asked the great and pioneering civil rights activist and former Georgia state senator, the Honorable Horace Julian Bond, what set of values and life expectations pushed him to serve his community while in college. In response, Hon. Bond suggested to me,

> I only looked to do what I saw my mother and father do on a daily basis. They read the newspaper and a book every single day. They were both educators and social activists in the sense that they sought to change minds in the classroom and in the library. They understood that if their service to the community could change the mind of a person, that person would then change the social behavior of someone else. Their system of values was transferable. I picked up their outlook on life as a child, and I've found those values were what encouraged me to excel in my undergraduate work as a student and what ultimately led to my participation with the Student Nonviolent Coordinating Committee (SNCC). I served the cause for freedom and justice because I had to.[1]

Isn't Bond's testimony of service inspiring? Perhaps your upbringing differs somewhat from that of the Honorable Julian Bond's. Maybe you didn't see the same social conscious and work ethic demonstrated by your parents on a daily basis. Nevertheless, if we are going to continue our discussion about what it means to be African American, Christian, and in college, we cannot do so without highlighting your commitment to service in the community.

You're now in your junior year of college, and you should be a bit more settled with the way things work on campus. You have your study habits down. You have established a trusted circle of friends. You might even have a special companion with whom you share a closer romantic relationship. And I pray that by now you have found the church that works best for you. So, let's talk about connecting in community.

Why? Whether you plan to pursue a career in your field or apply to graduate school after graduation, you will need to demonstrate some level of involvement in community service. Head knowledge gained in the ivory tower of academia only counts for so much in the real world. Employers and admission committees want to see that you cared enough about the world to apply the knowledge you are accumulating.

Here are a few observations I've made along my academic journey. Hopefully these insights can help you in determining how you desire to serve your community.

Student Government Associations (SGAs)

Most SGAs offer student-leaders the opportunity to represent their social class year—transfers, commuters, and resident students—on a variety of issues related to diversity and inclusion. If you have a strong desire to affect policy on campus, joining a SGA will offer you a great opportunity to serve your constituency—namely, your peers.

Campus Ministry

Most colleges offer a campus ministry through which the student body can offer faith-based outreach to the local community. Doing voluntary community service through campus ministry can provide you with rich opportunities to work with organizations such as Habitat for Humanity and the Special Olympics. Such organizations love to form relationships with this type of ministry. (The Christian fellowship within campus ministry is usually rich as well.)

Civic Engagement Center

Some colleges offer a community service center to train students in how to envision their citizenship in a global community. I find centers, such as Spelman's Center for Leadership and Civic Engagement, to be very inspiring. You may be able to receive a scholarship through this type of organization to participate in a grassroots project in another country.

Work-Study Programs

I know what you're thinking: How does a work-study program qualify as community service? These programs offer more than just jobs in the cafeteria or the mailroom. A good program will also offer opportunities for you to tutor rural or inner-city kids. Some programs will afford you the chance to build lower-income housing for residential redevelopment districts within your local community. Work-study positions such as these can be a great way to earn a little cash *and* gain the personal enrichment of getting involved with serving your college community's needs.

Reserve Officers' Training Corps (ROTC)

There are many different types of ROTC programs, but most of them are really good. Not only do they offer scholarships to students who desire to enlist as officers in the military upon graduation, but they also empower you for civil service through a multitude of training regiments.

For instance, the United States Air Force ROTC offers its college students a Leadership Laboratory in which cadets study the anatomy of leadership, the qualities of a good manager, and the communication skills needed for long-term planning and execution.

NAACP

I argue that this is one of the most unrecognized community service and social justice advocacy organizations in the nation. Please find out whether or not your college has an NAACP chapter! If they do not, contact the NAACP Youth Division to find a way to start one. A good college chapter will offer opportunities to provide leadership and mentorship to local public schools and after-school programs. You will engage in public discourse as an advocate for social justice in your local community. Voter registration drives, after-school tutoring programs, healthcare education, antidiscrimination advocacy on campus, and the study of national civil rights issues are all a part of the NAACP college chapter experience.

Fraternities and Sororities

Many would argue against the inclusion of our historic fraternal organizations in this section, but I feel I must. You will be hard pressed to find a more upfront social organization on campus. American history provides countless examples of our fraternal organizations' contributions to social justice advocacy and community engagement. I will not join the debate as to whether or not one organization is more active in community service than the other. Such conversation is divisive, and I urge you to avoid this kind of temptation.

What is important is that you research the various chapters that exist on your campus. Find out which organizations seem best suited to your interests and character. Confirm that your campus chapter is engaged in community service, and take it from there. I promise you— you will find their commitment to the upliftment of our people to be empowering.

Whatever community with which you choose to partner, make the most of the opportunities the group offers. Make time in your schedule to build relationships with other members as well as to participate in events and activities. Keep in mind that not only do such opportunities deepen your character, enrich your college experience, and expand your personal horizons, but the partnerships you forge will also look impressive on a future résumé!

Note

1. Conversation between author and Hon. Horace Julian Bond, NAACP Annual Leadership 500 Conference, Destin, Florida, December 9, 2006.

12

Staying on Track

So let me ask you, How are you doing? I mean, how are you *really* doing? I know this whole college experience has probably been like a whirlwind for you—is it possible that you're well into your junior year already? Are you nervous about the potential prospects that stand before you? Or maybe you don't see the light at the end of the tunnel just yet. Well, let's slow it down a bit. Let's take a breather and do a bit of self assessment.

How are your relationships holding up—at home and at school? I need you to be honest with your assessment. How do you feel about your grades? Physically, are you maintaining a reasonable measure of health? Are you enjoying your church and your commitment to community service? Have you given any thought to graduation and beyond? Are you sure you're on track to graduate on time? (Is your answer to that final question a resounding, *"Huh?"* If so, you'll want to pay extra attention to the next chapter!)

Relationship Checkup

It should be evident by now that relationships are a crucial factor in your college journey. From the start, we have talked about the importance of the people in your life—for better and worse. So which is it? At this point in your undergraduate sojourn, what is the relational verdict: Are you better or worse for the people who are in your life?

- With whom are you spending your time, and what activities do you engage in together?
- In what ways might that time spent be considered an investment—through studying, support, and social development? How is it wasted time—an expense you can ill afford because it is detrimental to your academics, spirituality, and physical health?
- In what ways are your friends a help to you? How are they a hindrance?
- Is your special friend an encouragement or a temptation? How well do each of you honor the boundaries you have agreed upon for the relationship?
- Concerning your relationships back home—with family, childhood or high-school friends, and church leaders—with whom have you stayed in touch, and why?
- What new relationships have you forged through church and community activities? Have you made any quality connections? How do those connections influence you?
- What mentoring relationships are you pursuing, if any? What opportunities for such mentorships have you neglected to pursue?

Academic Checkup

You have reached the halfway mark of your undergraduate career. Whether it took you two years of full-time coursework or much longer on a part-time track, you are halfway toward your goal. There are two truisms about halfway status. The first is encouraging and says, "Well begun is half done!" Make a good start and you're well on your way to success! But the second is cautionary: "Well begun is but half done," warning that no matter how well you started, you still have a long way to go. Though paradoxical, these two statements are "truisms" because they are, in fact, both true. As you consider these questions about your academic achievements, be encouraged by what you have accomplished—and be cautioned that you still have your work cut out for you!

- Have you completed your core requirements—those introductory courses required by most liberal arts schools to give students a broad foundation of general knowledge? By junior year, those requirements should be fulfilled.

- Have you developed solid study habits—or do you still find yourself pulling all-nighters to finish that paper or cram for an exam?

- What is your current Grade Point Average (GPA)? If you don't know what that is or what *yours* is, you'd better ask someone! And if it is low, you might consider looking at summer school as an opportunity to bring up your average.

- How many courses do you still need to fulfill the requirements for your chosen major? (You *have* declared a major by now, haven't you? If not, this is the year to make that choice. You'll need to bring closure to that issue quickly.)

- Have you met recently with your academic advisor to confirm that you are on track for graduation? If not, make the appointment today! Whether you are aiming for next year or several years from now, the equivalent of junior year is a good time to evaluate the timeline you have set for yourself and to determine if you are still on pace.

Physical Checkup

Do not ever pursue academic excellence at the expense of your physical and mental health. What good will it do you to earn the A on that paper if you are too sick and tired to study for the test the following day? And think longer term than that. What good will it do to earn that degree with honors if you compromise your health and any hope for quality of life beyond graduation? Remember, the habits you form now will probably last for a lifetime.

- How are you feeling nowadays? How often do you miss class because of illness? Frequent colds, infections, or stomach bugs may indicate larger health concerns—such as exhaustion, excessive stress, malnutrition, and depression.
- When was your last physical exam? You should have one annually, even when you are away at school. Women, that includes a visit to your OB/GYN.
- Are you keeping up on your dental visits? Even if you can't make it to your dentist every six months, keep up on good dental hygiene—brushing and flossing at least twice daily. A good toothbrush and mouthwash will carry you a long way in any relationship. Trust me when I tell you!
- How would you characterize your typical diet? Are you getting your five-a-day fruits and vegetables, or do you tend to rely on sugar, carbs, and caffeine for your energy boosts?
- What about weight management? If you have gained or lost significant weight since starting college, you may be endangering your health. Visit the school medical center or call your doctor for advice about improving your eating and exercise routines.
- How often are you engaging in regular cardiovascular activity? Do you know what a treadmill or a bicycle is? When was the last time you went for a walk that wasn't between classes or between your room and the dining hall?

Spiritual Checkup

I pray that your self assessment thus far has yielded a predominantly encouraging picture—that you have succeeded in laying a solid foundation of relational, academic, and physical behavior patterns that you can continue to build upon. If there are areas that clearly need improvement, don't be discouraged. You still have time to correct your course. And a close look at your spiritual health is a great first step toward self reform.

- How are you coping with the colliding worldviews you have encountered? How do you react to a new thought, differing belief, or opposing opinion—with sincere curiosity and respect, with uncertainty and fear, or with intolerance and anger?
- How has your worldview changed because of your interaction with other people, cultures, and ideas?
- What kind of local church have you partnered with, if any? What kind of ministries have you become involved in?
- What new passion and vision has the Spirit birthed in you through your classes, your community involvement, your friendships, and your other experiences at college?
- In what ways have your dreams, plans, and sense of calling for the future been modified or clarified during the first half of your college career?
- How has your faith grown, deepened, or changed since venturing beyond the walls of the church and community in which you were born again? Are the changes for better or worse?

Depending on your answers to the questions in this chapter—and don't bother lying because you and God are the only ones listening and you both know the truth already!—you may need to make some radical changes before your college career spins you wildly out of control. The good news is that you still have time—and God is still there to help you!

13

Satisfying Your Requirements

In chapter 12, one of the questions I asked in the initial self assess-ment related to whether you were on track to graduate. If you have no idea how to answer that critical question, this chapter is right on time. After all, you're half-way to three-fourths done with your undergraduate education now! Let me give you a few pointers on what you need to do to ensure that you don't embarrass yourself come graduation time. Remember, the goal is for you to start smart—and finish strong.

Stick with What Counts

If you are a degree-seeking student, then you must understand that taking too many courses outside your major will foil any plan for graduating in a timely manner. For example, if you are majoring in premed, don't spend too much of your time taking courses on pho-tography. Or if you are majoring in African American history, you shouldn't take too many courses on rock climbing. That's not to say you can't or shouldn't take advantage of a liberal arts education by taking some electives that interest you. But don't indulge your curiosity at the expense of your academic program. Most of your courses should contribute to your degree program. For the full-time student, I suggest no more than one elective outside your major each semester—or per year, depending on how many credits you can handle at one time.

Credits Do Matter

Full-time students, be sure you are taking at least 30–36 credits per year (i.e., 15–18 credits per semester). If your major requires more than 120 credits for you to earn your degree, you will need to take more than 36 credits during the standard school year. Alternatively, maybe you need to think about summer school as an option to help you bulk up on credits.

Part-time students, you will set your own schedule when it comes to how many credits are feasible in a given semester, but be sure to consult regularly with your academic advisor as you plan your academic program. Course requirements have been known to change, and some programs will have time limits for completing the program.

Whether full-time or part-time, you should use your junior year to assess your progress. Don't just look at the number of courses you have taken. Look at the credits you have earned—the courses for which you have earned the necessary grade. Few colleges and universities will give you credit toward graduation for a course in which you earned less than a C. And also look at the specific courses to be sure they satisfy the requirements for your major. Did I mention the importance of an academic advisor at this point in your college career?

Hold Up the Standard

I advise that you pay close attention to the departmental standards in which your major has been declared. What do I mean? Make sure you are maintaining the necessary grade point average (GPA) to satisfy your department's standards. Sometimes the college will honor a certain minimum standard for you to retain your eligibility as a student, but your academic program may hold to a higher standard. That standard doesn't just apply to earning credit for an individual course but also applies to remaining eligible for that degree program. For example, the university may require a minimum GPA of 2.0 for returning students, but the economics department may demand a more stringent 2.5 GPA for its majors.

Consult with Your Academic Advisor

I have said it before, but this point deserves its own heading! Please, please, *please* check in with your academic advisor on a regular basis. Sit down and ask your advisor to review your transcripts over and over again. A good academic counselor will run a credit audit to ensure that all your degree requirements are being fulfilled. Your junior year is a pivotal one in that you still have time to correct your academic course heading, in the event you have lost your way.

Consult with the Head of Your Department

An academic advisor is a great resource, but he or she is a generalist when it comes to academic programs. By your junior year, you should also check with the head of your department. You may think you are on pace to graduate; your academic advisor may even assure you that all is well. But without consulting with the head of your department, you can never be sure.

I recall meeting the head of my undergraduate philosophy department late in my junior year, only to find out I had too many electives and not enough core requirements to complete my major. I had assumed one class would meet the criteria of another. I was wrong. I had to improvise accordingly. My senior fall semester was a mess because I did not stay on track during my earlier college years.

Register on Time

After consulting with your advisor and department head, make sure you are registered for next semester's classes well before the deadline for registration expires. That means you need to schedule those consultations early on in your junior year. Hear me on this. Meet with your people at first opportunity, and get your registration in as early as possible. That way, not only can you be certain of what courses you need, you also improve your chances of getting into that required course.

It's true that most colleges give preference to upperclassmen when it comes to limited space in core requirement courses. However, not everyone has bought this book, so there may be a lot of seniors jostling for those precious seats. Last-minute and late registrations often result in disappointment or panic if the class is already filled on a first-come, first-served basis.

In a pinch, you can ask your advisor to intervene for you, whether to get an exception to a missed deadline or to squeeze you into a closed course. But in my experience, advisors hate those kinds of requests. And trust me—they will let you know about their displeasure!

Declare Your Intent to Graduate

Here is another key nugget of advice for you. Pay close attention to your campus mailbox. Sometime during the second semester of your junior year, your school should send you a form that asks about your intention to graduate the following year. This form will start the bureaucratic process involved before the registrar can confirm that you have enough credits in the right courses to do so.

Note the importance of this piece of paper! If you do not submit it by the deadline, you will be ineligible to graduate the following year— no matter how many credits you have or how high your GPA is. And if you believe you have attained second-semester-junior-year status but do *not* receive that form, check with your academic advisor and college registrar. Something might be missing from your academic transcript that it failed to trigger the usual process.

Follow Through

The key to finishing strong is your follow through. Make sure that you are following up on all of your commitments and responsibilities as a college student. Most colleges and universities offer a checklist for each major that provides a detailed outline of their requirements for graduation. Compare that checklist to your transcript to ensure you have completed all of your core courses from freshman year on. Be sure you haven't missed completing some critical document or process along the way.

To be Christian while in college is to be responsible with all the tasks that God has given you. Such responsibility encompasses all aspects of your life, and academics are critically important among the rest. After all, you may be in college for more than one reason, but certainly a primary goal is that degree! Be a good steward of your education by finishing strongly what you began "smartly."

14

Remembering to Stretch

I watched a basketball game the other day and saw one of the most amazing dunks ever. I mean, this dunk should be recorded as one of the NBA's greatest plays. Lebron James executed a crossover at the top of the key, drove down the center of the three-second lane, rose up in the air off one leg, and rammed the basketball in the rim. What lay in his wake was a crossed-over Tracy McGrady at the top of the key and a dejected Yao Ming standing under the basket. The crowd and I went crazy because we had witnessed a six-foot-eight man bang the back of the hoop with a leather ball while jumping over another man who measured at seven feet six inches.

It was an incredible play, but I thought about it and realized a play like that doesn't just happen. Those of us in the crowd have a tendency to focus only on the star play, and we overlook the preparation that comes *before* the play. Lebron James couldn't have made that leap if he stepped onto the court cold. He spends hours before each game stretching his body to ensure that he remains fluid when he competes.

Much in the same way, we need to stretch our own bodies to ensure that we remain in the academic game. By your junior year, it's tempting to hunker down and drive toward the finish. Just brace yourself, keep your head in the books and your hands on the computer keys, and somehow you'll manage to survive until graduation. The problem is you're only halfway to your goal—or at best, two-third of the way! You can't possibly hope to hold that hunkered-down position for another one-and-a-half to two years, either mentally or physically!

Consider this a call to stretch. The good news is that stretching your body ensures good health, improved posture, and a fresher mind. You'll need all three to get through these final semesters of college.

What Stretching Will Do for You

- Relax your muscles. Stretching will enable you to ease the tension in tight muscles that tend to group together when we become stressed. There's nothing like hunching over a computer to write a 20-page paper that's due in 24 hours. Raising the arms toward the ceiling while seated enables the tense shoulder muscles to loosen—and the 30-second break that the stretch gives your eyes and brain is also a needed mental reprieve.

- Increase your circulation. Stretching also improves blood flow throughout the body. Try standing up and rolling your head around your shoulders. Then bend over and touch your toes without bending your knees. Do you feel a warmth wash through your body? That's your blood circulating in places that had become numb from so many hours sitting in one place.

- Improve your flexibility. Stretching on a regular basis helps you become more limber. It loosens your muscles and keeps them more pliable. And the more limber you are, the less stressed your body will feel when subjected to pressure. Think of a rubber band. If you use it on a regular basis, it will tend to remain supple and elastic. If you let it sit in a drawer or file for months and years, however, it will dry out and lose its elasticity. The next time you try to stretch it, it will break. Now think of your neuromuscular systems like that rubber band. Trust me—you want to practice stretching on a regular basis, lest you snap!

- Increase your strength and stamina. The more you stretch, the longer your muscles become. The longer your muscles become, the more oxygen they absorb. The more oxygen they absorb, the longer they function under duress. Muscles that are stretched frequently tend to sustain higher levels of energy for longer periods of time.

- Fortify your immune system. It's true. Health specialists suggest the more you exercise, the better you'll feel. Stretching is a form of exercise. Having a limber body promotes the production of healthy cells in the body because good circulation ensures that nutrients are being distributed to the muscles, joints, and tendons. The stronger your body becomes, the more quickly it will respond to infections and viruses. Your body tends to replenish itself better when it is relaxed, limber, and fueled with nutrients.

Good Stretching Habits

- Inhale and exhale smoothly. Improper breathing can lead to dizziness and in some cases fainting.
- Stretch fluidly. Sudden jerks could cause you to pull a muscle. The idea is to increase circulation and not shock the body.
- Stretch slowly. Avoid quick or erratic movements that could cause sharp pain or blunt trauma.
- Stretch consistently. Develop a routine that your body can follow. It should be simple and not too rigorous, something that you can repeat in the same way on a regular basis.
- Stress carefully. If you feel a twinge or excess pain, stop. I know personal trainers often use the slogan "no pain, no gain." However,

pain is your body's way of communicating that something is wrong. You should not experience pain when you stretch. If you do, make sure your physician examines the cause of the discomfort.

Great College Stretches

- Roll your wrists gently clockwise and then counter-clockwise. Culminate with widely spread fingers. This is a great exercise if you spend a lot of time in front of the computer keyboard. The movement can relax tension built up around the wrist joints.
- Place the balls of your feet against the floor and push with all your leg strength downward for 15 to 20 seconds. Release the pressure for 30 seconds, and repeat the exercise several times. I do this when I'm studying late at night at my desk. You will find the releasing of pressure to be very relaxing.
- Place the palms of your hands against the wall and push forward with all your might for 15 seconds. Release the pressure for 20 seconds and then repeat the process. This exercise is a great excuse to stand up after sitting for long periods, and you will also find that the tension in your shoulders begins to ease over time.
- Sit in a chair with your back in an upright posture and your hands flat on a desk. Use your buttock muscles to push up toward the ceiling. Then allow your buttocks to relax. Repeat this ten times, and you should feel your lower back begin to relax. The idea is to focus on good posture. In the process, you alleviate tension in the lower back area that could possibly distract you from reading and retaining important information.
- To alleviate tension headaches, tuck your chin into your neck as you bring your head upward to a position of military attention. Hold this stretch for 10 or 15 seconds. Depending on the severity of the tension, you may need to do this in five or ten slow, consistent repetitions.

As I stated earlier, stretching improves your health, posture, and state of mind. While you are in college, try to maximize the physical efficiency and performance of your everyday tasks. Such practices will undoubtedly carry over into your professional career, increasing your chances for success and healthy living. Remember to stretch, but do so wisely. Use patience and take your time. Again, the idea is to loosen muscles and ease tension.

Stretching will not change your body into Vin Diesel's or Halle Berry's, but it will certainly help you to manage stress. If Lebron James can stretch his body to prepare for NBA competition, we can do the same to prepare for next week's exam.

15

Casting the Vision

If you are looking for a wonderful account of how perseverance and vision can inspire a community, read the story of Bessie Coleman. Born in Atlanta, Texas, in 1892, Bessie Coleman, also known as "Brownskin Bess" and "Bess the Brave," became the first American woman of any ethnicity to receive an international pilot's license in 1921. Coleman's pursuit of the achievement speaks of perseverance. African American pilots were not allowed to earn such privileges in the United States during that time. In spite of that fact, Coleman started businesses, solicited the support of investors, learned French, and sailed to Le Crotoy Somme, France, where she fulfilled her vision and learned to fly. Coleman dared to move around the obstacles that appeared to be immovable. Vision enabled Coleman to accomplish her dreams.

What It Takes

Based on Bessie Coleman's example, it is evident that vision takes *perseverance, discipline,* and *determination.* Casting a vision for the future is one thing. Seeing the vision through requires something else. Vision casting requires a commitment to excellence. It requires an individual to be willing to defy the odds and step over or through the mountains that appear to be insurmountable.

As you consider your future beyond graduation, make sure that you dream big. You have invested all this time, energy, and money into an undergraduate education. What next? Let your vision stretch you. Cast big ideas into the air, but also be willing to back those ideas with a commitment to process and preparation. It is through the process of preparation that your vision will come to pass.

Think Big and Make It Plain

Habakkuk 2:2 tells us to "write the vision and make it plain" (KJV). Think big, but make it plain when you communicate it to others. In fact, one of the best ways to cast a vision is to communicate its content effectively. Take Habakkuk's advice and write your vision down. Stick it on your wall. Post it on your bathroom mirror. Talk about it as much as you can, both to yourself and to others.

Part of that vision is how you see yourself. Mohammed Ali would shout "I am the greatest" because he believed that he was. How do *you* see yourself? Do you see yourself as a doctor? Then write down what type of doctor you would like to become, and hang that description on the refrigerator. Then try to reach out to doctors who are successful in the field. Tell *them* how you envision yourself. They will respond to your bold declarations.

Live Out What You Say

Another way to cast your vision and make it a reality is to practice living it. Learn your discipline. Practice it through community service. Look for mentorship programs in the corporate sector that allow you to work side by side with successful professionals in the field. Sometimes a vision for success will become clearer when you practice the vision through serving someone else. The great biologist,

Dr. Ernest Everett Just (1883–1941) started out by assisting the prominent zoologist Frank R. Lillie in reporting the scientific process of the sandworm *Nereis*. Through his service to another, Dr. Just continued to mature in his vocation by becoming the premier cellular biologist of his era.

Work the Mountain

One of the greatest lessons I've ever learned came from The Reverend Martha Simmons, president and publisher of the quarterly preaching journal *The African American Pulpit*. Do you know what she told me? "Never let money stop you from walking into your destiny."

What is your vision beyond graduation? If you desire to apply to graduate school but remain fearful of the cost, apply anyway. God will find the resources. Reach out to the private sector. Search the Internet for grants. Talk to the graduate department about fellowship opportunities.

Whatever your vision, walk toward it with a determined mindset. Persistence and prayer will help you to overcome your mountain. You will undoubtedly run into obstacles as you seek your vision for success. You'll need to learn how to overcome those hindrances and stumbling blocks that obstruct your way. Jesus instructed us to speak to the mountain if we have the faith to make it move (Mark 11:22-23). So speak to your obstacle. Make it move.

Know the Length of the Journey

As I mentioned earlier, you need to research how long it should take to make your vision come to pass. You need a clear understanding of the timeline. Make sure you look at life through a realistic lens to ensure that you don't build up false expectations that lead to disappointment down the road.

For instance, if you desire to become a chemical engineer, most bachelor's degree programs in engineering require four years, and most students find that it takes longer than that to complete their studies. Of course, then you'll need to go to graduate school, which requires a minimum of two to four years. So don't assume that you'll head the chemical engineering department at the University of Michigan without putting in a minimum of nine years of academic work and cutting-edge scholarship.

You get the point? As you cast your vision, make sure you understand the length of the journey required to make it come to pass.

Action Tips for Vision Casting

- Use your MySpace or Facebook blog page. According to the Job Outlook 2007 Fall Preview, employers are viewing profiles on Internet social networking sites to determine the competence and quality of potential recruits. Internet technology can be a helpful tool to promote your ideas and concerns for the community.

- Tell everybody what you hope to become. Good ideas are always contagious. The more you talk about an idea, the greater the probability that it will come to pass. And you never know who you might be talking to—and who that person might know! He or she might be in a position to help you make the vision real!

- Attend as many leadership conferences as you can. Leadership is "caught" as much as it is "taught." The best way to learn how to become a visionary is to hang around visionary people. Leadership events are a great place to meet dynamic leaders.

- Write down everything. Before you go to bed, write down the brilliant ideas that have come your way. Usually when things get quiet late at night, you can hear yourself think a bit better. Use this time to focus on what God may have revealed to you earlier in the day.

- Pray. Make sure that you pray for wisdom. Ultimately, it will be wisdom that will guide you toward success.

SENIOR YEAR

Getting Ready

16

Cementing Relationships

Isn't time amazing? Here you are in your senior year of college, and you probably look back and marvel. Perhaps it seems like only yesterday when you first arrived on campus. Or perhaps you have been plugging away at this college thing part time, and it feels like a lifetime since you earned those first credits. Whether time flies or flags, you finally have the finish line in your sights.

In your freshman year, you were focused on finding your way to class and cafeteria and navigating the new world you had entered. Sophomore year, you were concerned with disciplining your study habits and discerning the wannabees from your real friends. By your junior year, you glimpsed the future beyond college and began to worry about whether you had enough credits to graduate.

Your senior year creates its own kind of anxiety. You're trying to juggle details concerning cap and gown orders with midterms and papers—and oh yeah, talks with the career counselor about job interviews or grad school applications. It's enough to drive you crazy! Well, settle down a bit. Let's take our time—like Chris Brown on a slow R&B joint—and figure out how to make it through this last year together. Let's start with how we can cement the relationships that mean the most to us.

To Halve or to Hold?

No, that heading is not a typo. If you have been successful in cultivating a relationship with a special companion during these undergraduate years, chances are you both are experiencing anxiety about the future. What will happen to your special friendship after graduation? Will you choose to part from your "other half" or will you decide to hold on to this relationship and make it "official"? The following are issues you need to discuss together—and only you, your friend, and the Holy Spirit can provide the answers that are right for you.

- After graduation. What are your plans for the next 1–5 years? Will you go directly into the job market or pursue graduate studies? Are you planning to stay local, go where the job or education is, or return to your hometown? What are your friend's plans?
- Intentions. All things being equal, what are your intentions toward your companion? How serious are you about a long-term relationship? Are you just having fun while you walk this leg of the journey together—or do you intend to make future decisions that center, at least in part, around this person?
- Family. Have you met the parents yet? Has your companion met your family? Have the families been introduced to one another? How do each of you feel about the other's parents—and how do the parents feel about you? (Keep in mind: No one stands alone. We all came from somewhere, and we carry baggage—some good and some bad—from our family of origin.)
- Marriage. If your intentions are long-term, will you get married immediately after graduation, or will you wait a few months or even years until your futures are more secure—after your friend has a secure job or you complete your graduate studies?

Tips for Treading Deep Relational Waters

If you weren't nervous about the next steps in your special relationship before, you should be now! These are some big questions, and the answers can affect the rest of your life. The future is scary stuff—but be strong and courageous. Trust that God has your future in hand, and the Spirit will give you (and Lord willing, your friend) wisdom to walk into that future together—or to part ways when your roads diverge in the proverbial wood.

May I add that part of being strong and courageous in this area means being man or woman enough to initiate the conversation? Sure, the discussion may be tense and awkward, especially if you have not discussed these issues in the past—and particularly if you and your friend do not immediately see eye to eye on the decisions to be made. In a spirit of empathy—I've been there, done it myself!—I offer these general suggestions for keeping your head above water as you tread where many fear to go!

- Be honest. Whatever conclusions you have come to in your own heart, keep it real with your special friend. Explain how you feel and what your intentions are. You might even map out a rough plan of what you intend to do in the near future—and where, if at all, you see that companion in that future.

- Meet the parents. If you haven't already done so, request a meeting with your special friend's family—especially with Mom and Dad (or whoever raised your friend). Even if you aren't decided on marriage, meeting the family can offer insight that may be helpful in making the decision. Especially if you *have* set your sights on "til death do us part," reveal the depths of your heart to your friend's parents. Brothers, let the parents know your desire to marry their daughter. Ask for their permission to proceed with your plan. Sisters, if you know where this relationship is headed, give your parents fair warning—and let his folks know how much he means to you. If either set of parents ask you to wait, I recommend that you respect their wishes. God has a purpose for every temporary setback.

- Ask the question. I suggest finding a common space that you and your special friend often share—a favorite park, a quiet lounge, a special restaurant. Then, when you are private and comfortable, ask your companion—not if he or she *will* marry you but if marriage is a future he or she can envision sharing with you. A familiar place may cultivate a sense of safety when you make your first foray into new emotional territory.

- Stick with the plan. If your intention is to wait until after graduate school, wait until after graduate school. If you agree to wait until both of you find a job, wait until both of you land a job. Don't allow insecurity, fear, or—yeah, I'll say it plain—lust, tempt you to take shortcuts. You made your decision carefully and prayerfully. Trust the wisdom God gave you, and in the Lord's perfect time, your success will make room for you and the person whom you love.

Cementing Your Foundational Friendships

I hope that you have made some lifelong friendships with a handful of quality peers on campus. They were the ones who bailed you out when you ran out of cash. They covered for you when you ducked out on a strange person in a strange situation. Or maybe they had your back and pulled you through that hated class when you just couldn't get it. When your childhood pet died or former love interest got married (to someone else), they stuck by and helped you work through the stages of grief in your own way. These types of friends are hard to come by. Cherish these relationships, and do what you can to ensure that such quality persons remain in your life beyond your college career. Here are just a few suggestions for doing just that.

- Take your friend out. Buy your favorite lounge rat a coffee at Starbucks. Treat your faithful study partner to a decadent dessert at the local diner. Surprise your roommates with a dinner and movie of their choice. It's a great opportunity to spend a little more quality time together. And while you're out, seize the chance to tell your friends how much you appreciate their support and commitment.
- Exchange contact information now. Personal (non-campus) e-mail addresses and cell phone numbers are probably the least likely to change, but be sure to exchange family snail mail addresses and phone numbers as well. Even as jobs change, education progresses, and marriages happen, your friend's parents are almost certainly going to keep tabs on their child!
- Give a token of friendship. For men, a Waterman pen or a stylish power tie is a gift that recognizes your friend's sterling character. For women, a quality piece of jewelry or silk scarf in her favorite color communicates the value of her integrity. Any friend will appreciate the significance of your gift of a new leather study Bible with a message of gratitude and encouragement inscribed in its flyleaf.

From College Mentor to Lifelong Friend

One of the best experiences you'll ever have as a student is when you contact your favorite professor or coach a few years after college graduation. There's nothing more fulfilling than recognizing how your professor's mentorship has come to life in your daily travel. And trust me, professors love to see their students prosper. When they witness the emergence of leadership in your life, it validates their commitment to the teaching profession. Here are just a few suggestions for staying connected with your mentor before and after graduation.

- Tap their knowledge—and I mean outside the classroom. Include professors in your discussions regarding a job search or the appropriate graduate school. Ask coaches or advisors about juggling competing interests and priorities. I've found that relationships grow as people share common interests and information. Include your mentors in the decisions that you make. They've been there and done that. That's why they are mentors.

- Express yourself. Before commencement or soon after, send your favorite mentor some flowers, a thank-you card—even a quality baseball cap from the Negro Baseball League. You get the point? It doesn't matter what token you choose. What matters is that you express your gratitude to the mentors who have shaped the way you think and interact with society. And remember: If you plan to go to graduate school, you will need endorsement letters! So it behooves you to remain cordial with your mentors.

- Stay in touch. On a regular basis after graduation, drop your professor an e-mail or call your coach. Most mentors enjoy hearing from their mentorees with news about major life events or even just a casual inquiry about life on campus. And you never know. Your mentor may need your assistance with a new project. It would be an honor to serve alongside the persons who have made such tremendous contributions toward your transition from college to "real life"!

The Power of a Thank-You

No matter which relationships mean the most to you, make sure that you express your appreciation for what they have contributed to who you are today. All the individuals God sent into your life deserve to be thanked for their commitment to you and their influence on your development. You are in your senior year of college, not just because you deserve to be there, but because an entire village of people helped you along the way. Remember to honor those who make sacrifices for you. Honor your pastor. Honor your professors. Honor your friends and family, and honor God. Remember to say thank you.

17

Keeping Both Eyes on the Prize

I have a paper due tomorrow. However, I can't seem to break away from a bizarre rerun that has captured my attention. There's nothing worse than a two-timing person who portrays him or herself as a devoted partner in a relationship. In this particular episode of *Girlfriends,* Joan (Tracee Ellis Ross) has fallen in love with her unemployed boyfriend's agent. Their assignations are scandalous, and neither one of them is prepared to tell the boyfriend that he is the odd man out. You would think somebody would come forward for the Lord's sake, but neither culprit to the crime confesses the transgression. You may ask why I should care. Why would I be concerned with the affairs of Tracee Ellis Ross? Well, the answer is quite simple: I've got senioritis. *I'm* a senior in graduate school, and I've totally lost focus.

You Must Finish the Race

I'm quite sure that by now you are tired of writing papers and reading dense chapters on subject matter that bores you. You've hit a brick wall on your senior thesis, and everybody seems to get on your nerves. You aren't alone. I've been there and done that. I can remember times when I would defiantly neglect an assigned reading just for defiance sake. I'd log onto ESPN.com. I'd read *The New York Times* online, or I would play Pac-Man on the laptop. It's not that I didn't want to do the work. I was just plain ole tired of school and deadlines.

But you know what? A lesson to be learned from this journey is the process of finishing what you've started. Each of us must learn how to finish the race that we started. The moment you said yes to God and accepted your invitation to college, you made a promise that you cannot break. In case you have forgotten, here are a few reasons you should keep your eyes on the prize:

- More Degrees = More Paper. And by paper, I mean *paper*. People with academic degrees tend to earn more money than those without. If you calculate how this pay scale plays out over time, you'll find that the difference can translate into millions of dollars. And remember, whether you finish the degree or not, those college loans will come due just six months after graduation. Might as well earn that degree, position yourself to earn more paper, and pay off the debt a little sooner.

- More Degrees = More Opportunity. According to CNNMoney .com, in 2006 the top five fastest-growing careers in the nation were: 1) software engineer, 2) college professor, 3) financial advisor, 4) human resource manager, and 5) physician assistant. And you know what? You need a degree to advance in each of those vocations. Having a degree opens the door to career advancement more quickly than anything else. Please stay focused. You need your degree.

- More Degrees = More Value. If you get the chance, listen to the lyrics of Beyonce Knowles's hit single "Upgrade U." If you think the brother in the lyrics feels dissed, try working an entry level job with no degree. I can guarantee you someone in the front office is playing Beyonce's song. When it's time for management to upgrade the work force, who do you think is the first person out the door? The degree you earn today will speak volumes to a future employer about your character, ambition, and determination to finish what you start.

- More Degrees = More Confidence. Simply put, you'll feel a whole lot better about yourself when you finish this degree. Not only is it a relief to put the four years' or more worth of work behind you, but you will have tangible proof of an accomplishment. Like getting a driver's license or landing your first summer job, earning a degree is a rite of passage. For the traditional student, it marks a transition from adolescence to adulthood. For the nontraditional student, it is a trophy that declares your stamina and a symbol of your courage to pursue a dream.

Look, I know it's hard to maintain your pace as you head into the homestretch. Maybe you even feel as though you are paying for classes that you may never use in life. But not only will life surprise you by revealing the relevance of presumed trivia, but the education you gain in college is comprised of far more than the facts you memorize and the skills you hone. A huge facet of your education is wrapped up in the habits you form—and the commitments you honor.

Take encouragement from Paul, who declared, "Not that I have already obtained this or have already reached the goal; but I press on to make it my own, because Christ Jesus has made me his own. Beloved, I do not consider that I have made it my own; but this one thing I do: forgetting what lies behind and straining forward to what lies ahead, I press on toward the goal for the prize of the heavenly call of God in Christ Jesus" (Philippians 3:12-14, NRSV).

Let the Legacy Continue

Do you know why else you need to finish? You need to finish because so many of our people have shed blood, sweat, and tears so that we could get an education. If you have never done so, be sure that you view Henry Hampton's classic six-part documentary entitled *Eyes on the Prize*. The film captures the birth of the Civil Rights movement beginning with Rosa Parks's defiant protest against racial discrimination and Emmett Till's murder in 1955, and continues with focusing on key moments in the movement. The key events include Rev. Dr. Martin Luther King Jr.'s "I Have a Dream" speech capping the 1963 March on Washington, the Freedom March in Alabama, the rise of the Black Panthers, desegregation, and the emergence of Jesse Jackson's Operation PUSH.

If you know your history, there's really no way you can justify not finishing this process. Go back to chapter 14. Stretch a few times, and then get back at it. Your people wait for your becoming. Better yet, destiny waits for you. Keep both eyes on the goal. Graduation isn't that far away. Press on, my friend, and seize the prize!

18

Considering Your Options

Let's talk about options. I looked on the Internet the other day to see who the highest paid athlete in the world was. Can you guess? It might be easy to guess the highest paid male: Tiger Woods. But can you guess who the highest paid *female* athlete might be? Are you stumped? OK, I'll tell you. The emerging Russian tennis icon Maria Sharapova. In 2005 Sharapova made more than $19 million in endorsements alone.[1] As the fellas in the hood would say, "Sharapova got cake, yo!"

If you dig deeper into Sharapova's profile, you'll notice something very peculiar and very smart at the same time. Sharapova maintains nine different streams of income simultaneously. Did you hear me? I said *nine!* Nine different companies pay for her marketability as a tennis player. They market products to you and me using Sharapova's smile, eyes, and reputation to make a profit. You might ask why Sharapova would need nine different companies to pay the rent, but I think her handlers would give you an answer even I could understand: They like to have options.

Doing good business requires that we evaluate every opportunity that comes our way. If the opportunity proves to be fruitful to the head and the heart, then we should consider such an opportunity seriously. So let's talk about options in this chapter. What kind of options are you looking at in your senior year as you approach graduation?

Career Decisions: Door #1 or Door #2

I mentioned this point earlier in the book, but I'll say it again considering how important this insight has proven to be in my own life. *Go with your heart.* If you have to make a choice that you're uncertain about, go with your heart. Most college graduates are still uncertain about what they want to do with their lives after college. That's probably part and parcel of why I was asked to write this book: to help you find your way along the journey.

Don't be discouraged or daunted if you arrive at graduation and still don't know what you want to be when you grow up. Prayerfully, you have narrowed the field of choices, but finding your life's passion takes time. In fact, most experts suggest that college graduates change their career at least once before settling down into a vocation they feel passionate about. Look at me. I went from being a multiplatinum record producer to studying at the University of Oxford and Princeton Theological Seminary. What can I say? When you follow your heart, *God* stuff happens.

Choosing a Graduate School

For many of you, pursuing the PhD or the MBA isn't an option. Fulfilling your dream and achieving your calling means you have to go on to graduate school. Well, let me give you a bit of advice:

- Research the schools. Which schools offer the program you want? Which are located in the area you want or need to live? What are the entrance requirements, and what will you need to achieve to complete the program? Be sure the schools you decide on will meet your needs and fit your ambitions. Then apply to more than one!

- Identify the experts. Contact the professors with whom you desire to do research. Many of them will invite you to their campus to talk about your future at their college or university. Before your visit, read at least two books or articles that professor has written or edited. What professor will believe you are serious about working with her if you know nothing about her scholarship?
- Prepare for the test. Most graduate programs will require you to take the GRE or similar standardized test. Take my advice and pay for the tutoring class. Please do not go into the exam blind! As Arnold Schwarzenegger would say, "It 'vill break you." The same goes for the LSAT. Don't play with it.
- Take your time—but don't miss your deadlines! Take six months to a year to prepare, which may mean taking your GRE class while you are still completing your undergrad courses. Get all your paperwork in order and submit it well in advance of the posted deadline. And keep copies of everything, just in case something gets lost in the mail.
- Get strong recommendations. Every graduate school is going to ask for letters of academic and personal reference. Make sure your favorite professors and biggest fans are writing yours. However, do *not* allow the instructor who gave you a C- to comment on your scholarship, no matter how well you get along outside of class. Put your best foot forward—or stay at home!

Getting a J-O-B

First things first: What do you want to do? Granted, you may change careers a time or two before you settle into the vocation that perfectly suits your passions. (If you don't have a clue about a future profession by now, please don't tell the fiancé(e). You'll be on the shelf until you can figure it out!) Remember, a college degree *and* a plan will carry you a long way. A degree with no plan leads to the night shift at Burger King. I'm serious. So, take these suggestions seriously.

- Write down what you want to do and where you want to do it. If you live in the North but long for warmer climes, make sure you're flooding the South with applications and requests for interviews.

- Take advantage of Career Day on campus. Most colleges and universities invite corporate and private sector employers to their campuses to showcase their talent pool. Make sure that you are in that pool and swimming strongly—dressed well, with updated résumés printed and ready to hand out. Bring your calendar, too, just in case someone requests a meeting right then and there!

- Hit the Internet. Don't just post your résumé on the major Internet job sites. Search the websites of the companies for which you desire to work and contact them. If you prefer a diverse workforce, then look for companies that promote diversity. Make sure you don't miss regional recruitment dates. Sometimes a corporation may not visit your school, but its representatives will be in the area. Do your homework.

- Make sure your résumé and cover letter are tight. Do not send anything handwritten to an employer or you and your portfolio will be circular filed like a fake gold chain—in the garbage, OK? Ask a professor or academic advisor to help you. Hire a professional if you have to. One of the first lessons I learned while serving the prestigious New Jersey Amistad Commission as a graduate fellow was how to structure a résumé. Yes, I had a college degree and I still needed help with my stuff, so don't be afraid to ask for help.

- Interview strongly. Dress for the job you want. Appearances *do* count. Women and men, dress conservatively in a navy blue suit. Men, find a power tie and shine your shoes. Leave off the earrings, and go bare-knuckled. Ladies, choose a modest neckline and skirt that's longer than your fingertips, or wear a classy pantsuit. Wear the heels you would walk to church in, not stroll the clubs. Take off the "bling bling," and put away the MP3 ear buds. Silence your cell, pager, and any other gadgets you carry. Visit the barber or beauty shop to be sure your hair is in order. Take a shower and brush your teeth, and then pop a mint while you're waiting in the lobby. Make eye contact and sit up straight when you're offered a seat. *Please* do not chew gum during the interview.

The "Navi" or the SLSC

Undoubtedly you will come across the one question that we all ask ourselves when we approach graduation. If I get hired by Johnson & Johnson or Merck, will I buy the "Navi" now or will I pay off my student debt? You know what my response is going to be, so don't even ask. Please work on your debt if you have any. Remember, Student Loan Servicing Center (SLSC) will start calling six months after you graduate from college. The average college student owes about $30,000 upon graduation. Leave the "Navi" alone. It will depreciate as soon as you drive it off of the lot anyway. If you can afford to buy a big-ticket item, buy a house and develop some equity. Otherwise, knock off your debt and keep on moving. You don't want to start off your new life after college the wrong way.

You knew college and that degree would open up whole new worlds of opportunity to you. Now that you're on the brink of the future, be sure that you choose wisely. And don't forget the value of the people, prayer, and patience that have brought you this far! Ask for help, pray for wisdom, and pace yourself lest panic or passivity force you to accept a future you will reject for years to come.

Note

1. www.forbes.com/lists/2005.

19

Creating Habits for a Lifetime

As graduation draws closer and closer, you'll need to start thinking about which habits you'll want to bring with you and which habits need to be thrown to the wayside. We're talking about quality of life issues here. The way you like to dress, eat, stretch, run, sleep, and the like. As I mentioned earlier, college is as much about developing good habits as it is about learning information. The idea behind college is that you become knowledgeable of your humanity and the boundaries of your human existence.

One of the greatest testimonies I can give you on how good habits come about would come from my personal experience in watching the star of the highly acclaimed TV sitcom *Everybody Hates Chris,* Tyler James Williams, grow as a young man in Jesus Christ. While many of you may know Tyler Williams in character as Chris Rock, a swash-buckling teenage survivor from the streets of Bed-Stuy, New York, I know Ty as himself. As the former youth minister of Bronx Christian Fellowship, I know the Tyler Williams who would come to children's church in the Bronx with a Bible in hand every Sunday.

And I mean *every* Sunday. He's been singing "This little light of mine, I'm gonna' let it shine" since he was five years old! And you know why? Because his momma and daddy (who are both pastors now) love the Lord. And they taught Tyler how to love the same God they've known all the days of their lives. They instilled their own habits in him—and he is carrying those habits through his own adolescence, and college years.

Creating good habits that last a lifetime takes forethought. You have to make up your mind how you want to live your life. And then you have to follow through on those decisions.

The Thinking Mind

If there is one thing you should take away from your college experience, it's an ability to think critically on the issues of life. When I talk about thinking, I'm not talking about the simple regurgitation of facts. I'm referring to a disciplined process of seeking information, processing it, weighing your opinion and others against the facts, and coming to a sound, informed conclusion concerning your position on a matter. You see, some minds never move far beyond what science calls our "autonomic functions"—those unconscious physical functions such as the heart pumping blood and the lungs processing oxygen. Such a mind never engages the higher levels of thinking. Oh, it may consider what is necessary to survive, but it does so only with short-term goals and no consideration of the bigger picture.

In contrast, a thinking mind will travel the expanse of the globe, considering how a specific action taken in this corner of the world will affect the larger human community. A thinking mind will demonstrate curiosity beyond its own egocentric existence. A thinking mind will apply the facts it accumulates and extrapolate from today's reality into a future only dimly imagined.

Good Health

As I have stated throughout this handbook, good health is a key to success. Watching your diet, maintaining an exercise routine, getting enough sleep, and practicing regular stretching all lead to a sound mind and a willing body. You cannot maximize your life's potential without taking your health into consideration. Remember to make an appointment for your annual physical. Visit the dentist. In fact, go to the student health center the moment you read this paragraph. The last thing you want to do is graduate with bad health if you can help it. Take your health seriously and your body will take you seriously. As my college coach would say, "You cannot make withdrawals from a bank that has no funds." So make sure you make healthy deposits into your body bank.

Rest Is Not Negotiable

We talked about this in chapter 9, and I'll emphasize it again here. If you think the demands of college have taken a toll on your sleep schedule, you haven't seen anything yet! Establish habits of getting adequate and consistent rest—and not just with 8 hours of sleep each night. God himself set aside a day of rest after the work of Creation was done. Are you more capable than God? Be sure to set aside a sabbath for yourself. Do not fall into the cultural trap of thinking that success can only come when you burn the candle at both ends. You shall surely perish. You may not feel the effects of sleep deprivation now, but you *will* feel its effects later.

I recall studying for a presentation on "The Philosopher David Hume: The Problem of Evil and Contemporary Suffering through the Hermeneutical Lens of Job." Sounds deep, right? The presentation dealt with the reason for suffering in the twenty-first century, but it taught more about suffering than I anticipated. In my zeal to prepare for the presentation, I hadn't slept for three days. And you know what happened? I passed out. When I got back to my apartment on campus, my body crashed and it took me more than a week to recover.

Please do not make the mistake I did. Rest your body. What good is it to be known as a world renowned scholar if you pass away before your prime?

The Necessity of Work

If you do not work, you will not eat, plain and simple. No matter how talented or gifted you are, if you do not learn how to manage a healthy work ethic you will not prosper in this life. I don't care if you know how to dunk a basketball. Someone in Lithuania can jump higher than you. And I could care less if you can sing the paint off the walls of your church. Trust me—my home church has more singers than Billie has holidays. The gifts will not do you any good if you are not exercising them with a disciplined ethic of work.

The Bible calls it good stewardship—and the principle is governed by natural consequences. Imagine a parent who repeatedly tells a child, "Don't touch the stove; it's hot" only to have to keep snatching the child's hand away from the stove's surface. So the next time the child reaches out, the parent keeps still and lets the child experience the heat for him or herself. The mild burn is a natural consequence.

You ought to be mature enough to heed a warning, but if not, prepare for the natural consequence. God has given each of us a work to do, and that work will enable you to provide for yourself, your family, and your future. If you are unwilling to use the privileged gifts God has deposited in you, you will perish from a lack of sustenance. Work is a gift from God. *Enjoy* working. By working in your gifts, you will be empowered to stretch beyond yourself and contribute to making provision for all of society.

Essential Worship

Of all the lifelong habits you form, none is more important than establishing a custom of worshipping God for all that the Lord has done. If you took me seriously in chapter 10, you have connected with a local congregation and been faithful in fellowship, service, and worship. Such faithful involvement in Christ's Body is probably the greatest life lesson you can learn in college. If you cannot master any other habit, master this one. Learn to find a place of worship wherever you go. In fact, learn to worship God every waking moment of your life on earth.

The psalmist instructs us, "Make a joyful noise to God, all the earth; sing the glory of his name; give to him glorious praise" (Psalm 66:1-2, NRSV). Remember to make a joyful noise to God. Thank God for pulling you through those demanding courses in political science, statistics, and physics. Sing glory to God for keeping you in good health. Give God praise for allowing you to graduate with honors, in spite of the harmful words people may have spoken about you.

You are on your way! Look at what the Lord has done. If you can't remember anything else about your college experience, remember to give God praise. Praise should go with you all the days of your life.

20

Ending as You Mean
to Begin (Again)

And here we are. You've made it. You're packing boxes in your room at Spelman College for the last time. People are calling you on the cell left and right as you walk along the quad at the University of Syracuse. The G. R. Little Library at Elizabeth City State University is demanding its books back. You've cracked your last jokes with your favorite custodian and security guard at the Community College of Allegheny County. Even the dining services staff at Virginia Union is getting teary-eyed. These are your last days on campus, and you just don't know how to act.

I can understand the space that you're in. There's nothing like taking that last exam. I mean that *last*, last exam, especially if that one exam determines whether you graduate or return to summer school. There's a feeling of elation that fills your spirit, something that causes your nerve endings to tingle. You don't know what to do with yourself, but you know that you've accomplished something great. And you did. *You have earned your college degree.* Nobody gave it to you. You earned it. The only advice I can offer you at this moment of pure euphoria is this: End this thing the way you started it.

Make New Goals

Remember how you arrived on campus and you began to construct the goals you would seek to accomplish throughout your college career? Well, guess what? You'll need to draft an entirely new set of goals for life after graduation. Focus on what you want to accomplish in one year and in five. Will you attempt to climb the corporate ladder, or do you want to take a teaching job instead? Or perhaps you desire to establish yourself as an entrepreneur. What plan do you have in place to fund your vision? Have you talked to anyone about your dream—people who might be prospective partners or investors? Planning to go straight to grad school? I hope you have all your applications in and your financial aid in place! If you have thoughts of children and marriage, what time frame are you working in? Have you talked to your special companion about your intentions and timeline? Remember what I stated earlier: You'll need to cast your vision outward to see it come to pass. That goes for personal as well as professional visions.

Invest in a Wardrobe

OK, this is a critical piece that many traditional college students overlook. When you arrived on campus, you had a few clothing items to be proud of. Maybe you loved your favorite white J-Lo Puffer Jacket or a pair of Sean John Blacks a.k.a El Morenos. Everywhere you turned your friends were shouting you out, "Yo! Holla at ya' boy!"

Well, guess what? It's time to fold the Puffer Jacket away and put the El Morenos back in the sneaker box. Men and women alike, you'll need several dark-colored suits and several pairs of good conservative shoes. You are a working professional now. You have a new standard to live by, and everyone who has supported you these last four years or more looks for you to carry it out to the fullest. You can ask any of my friends how important this topic is to me. You should have timeless pieces in your closet that will never go out of style. A good pea coat will never let you down. I'm not telling you to throw away the throwback jersey. I'm only asking that you save it for the barbeque. Remember what we talked about in chapter 18: You have to dress for the job—and the life—that you want.

Let Your Last Goodbyes Be Classy

You may never meet many of your classmates and professors again—but you never know. So, let your goodbyes be classy. Please do not end your acquaintances with simple head nods and grunts. If you are ending a relationship with that special companion, make sure that you thank him or her for the good times you did have. Even in the dark moments, you learned something about yourself and you learned something about the nature of people.

Also, make sure that you stop by your professors' offices to let them know how much they mean to you. You might even lead a standing ovation at the conclusion of a final lecture. Shake your mentors' hands. Look them in the eye and tell them how much of an impact they have made in your life. This type of initiative will separate you from the ill-informed or the calloused of heart.

And make sure you send a letter to the president of your college. Let that individual know that you appreciate his or her leadership. You would be surprised how many college presidents are depressed because they really can't gauge whether they are making an impact on the lives of the students for whom they are responsible.

Clean Your Room

Respect the college property and restore it to the condition in which you found it—or better. If you painted your dorm room pecan brown, please make a trip to Home Depot or Lowes, buy off-white paint, and repaint your room. Clean the bathroom and vacuum the carpet. If your mattress is covered in vinyl, wash that down as well. If your campus apartment has a kitchen, clean it and ensure that any equipment you leave behind is complete and in good working order. Please do not leave that responsibility to your parents or the college administration. It wouldn't be right for you to leave behind your burnt scallopped potatoes on the stove for someone else to clean. You have heard the expression, "The devil is in the details"? Trust me. People are always looking to see whether or not you are going to blow your Christian witness. Stewardship of what belongs to someone else is a critical part of that witness.

Walk the Aisle with Your Ancestors

Most important, remember your ancestors as you march toward your degree certificate during the commencement service. Remember them as your name is called. Remember them and honor them with a tear or a moment of silence. They died in their toil so that you could stand before nations. Remember the historic contributions your African people have made in American history. Remember those who persevered through great odds to earn their degrees. Maya Angelou is watching you. Hon. Julian Bond is watching you. Mohammed Ali is watching you. Art Tatum is playing a riff from the pearly gates of heaven. Richard Wright is recording your story. Sarah Vaughan is leading solo to the tune that you've set as you walk down the aisle.

God bless you. You have stayed the course, and you have finished this leg of the journey. Worship God. Celebrate with family. Enjoy the moment. For today is a good day, as fleeting as it may be. And tomorrow is but a rising dawn away.

Looking Beyond

Thirty-one years ago, in September 1975, I began my journey as an undergraduate at Geneva College in Beaver Falls, Pennsylvania. I would eventually transfer, attend, and graduate from Eastern University in St. Davids, Pennsylvania. I entered both institutions with mixed emotions. I did not know many people, I was unsure of where things were, and I was not immediately comfortable with my surroundings. However, in time I learned where the library and the chapel were. In fact, both places became close friends. (To be really honest, so did the pizzeria downtown!) I came to know people and developed good solid friendships. I found myself mixing with a crowd that really wanted to "go forth" not only academically, but also in the Lord. Some of those friendships I still have today.

Regrettably, there are so many who begin their college journey who simply do not finish. It is not that they lack the intellectual ability. Many do not finish because they make poor choices, possess poor study habits, neglect a healthy routine, and fail to manage the responsibility of work, play, prayer, and practice. Far too many of us feel that it is not cool to be smart, and some have chosen to be dumb on purpose. As Christopher Michael Jones has said in his first book, *What to Expect When You're Accepted,* "Like-minded people attract like-minded people. If you walk or talk trash, you will attract trash." So many have fallen by the wayside, disqualified themselves, and did not finish their academic journey, not only because they lacked "wind beneath their wings," but because they lacked the essential tools that were necessary in making the transition into college life easier.

Rev. Christopher Michael Jones has provided you with a short practical handbook not only on how to survive your college years, but how to come through successfully! With great care he has offered step by step instructions for each year of college from getting settled, to getting serious, to getting ahead, to getting ready. Particularly in the early chapters, he put great emphasis on spending time in the library, maintaining balance, getting appropriate rest, and more importantly maintaining an appropriate prayer life. On one of the greatest journeys of your life, I feel confident this book will serve you well.

You, sons and daughters, are the generation to whom we will pass the torch, for whom our ancestors bled and died. Indeed, you will carry the message that "the God of our weary years and the God of our silent tears has brought us thus far on the way." As the Lord spoke to Joshua, "Joshua, Moses my servant is dead; now you take it from here," this first work will help you indeed to "take it from here." You will need mental, spiritual, and moral strength to withstand the dangers, fears, difficulties, and pressures of life to venture out and go forward. Your generation faces great temptation, including the temptation to be dumb on purpose. It has been said that "Courage in people is like a tea bag. You never know their strength until they are in hot water."

It is clear to me that this work will assist you in walking through your college experience with courage and dignity. Maya Angelou has said, "Courage may be the most important of all virtues because without it, one cannot practice the other virtues with consistency." Jesus himself has said a house that is built upon a rock will stand, but a house that is built upon a shore will fall when storms come (see Luke 6:48–49). I am confident that this critical tool will assist you in the midst of every storm. For this his first book, I commend my beloved son in the faith and ministry, Rev. Christopher Michael Jones, elder at Cathedral International, emerging Fulbright Scholar at Princeton Theological Seminary, and one of the winners of *The African American Pulpit*'s 2006 "Best Seminarians' Sermon Contest." I sincerely believe that he holds a bright light for our future as one of the emerging prophetic, prolific, and sincere voices of our time. He will speak truth to power and give us all hope to make it farther into the Promise Land.

Press on, young people, press on! Exude character, moral excellence, and strength. Do what is right; guard your reputation; be honest; be true to your word; be sensitive to the needs of others; allow God to direct your steps, and take the name of Jesus with you everywhere you go.

It's your turn! The same God that was with Abraham, Isaac, Jacob, and Joseph, Moses and Joshua, Peter and John, Paul and Silas, Mary and Dorcas, Harriet Tubman and Sojourner Weaver, Martin Luther King and Thurgood Marshall, Mother Teresa and Desmund Tutu, is the same God who is with you. Remain committed, and stay the course. Never give up; hang in there; the Lord will make a way.

Thank you, Rev. Christopher Michael Jones, for this much needed work. It is not only a sound and solid read, but it offers a voice of direction and solid inspiration for the next generation.

Rev. Dr. Donald Hilliard Jr.
Senior Pastor, Cathedral International
Presiding Bishop
Covenant Ecumenical Fellowship and Cathedral Assemblies
December 9, 2006